BIBLE PROPHECY
for Kids

REVELATION 1-7

KAY ARTHUR
JANNA ARNDT

HARVEST HOUSE PUBLISHERS

EUGENE, OREGON

Scripture quotations in this book are taken from the New American Standard Bible®, © 1960, 1962, 1963, 1968, 1971, 1972, 1973, 1975, 1977, 1995 by The Lockman Foundation. Used by permission. (www.Lockman.org)

Illustrations by Steve Bjorkman

Cover by Left Coast Design, Portland, Oregon

SUSTAINABLE FORESTRY INITIATIVE
Label applies to the text stock

Certified Sourcing
www.sfiprogram.org
SFI-00341

BIBLE PROPHECY FOR KIDS

Copyright © 2006 by Precept Ministries International
Published by Harvest House Publishers
Eugene, Oregon 97402
www.harvesthousepublishers.com

ISBN 978-0-7369-1527-4 (pbk.)
ISBN 978-0-7369-3554-8 (eBook)

Printed in the United States of America

12   13   14   15   16   17   /ML-SK/   12   11   10   9   8   7   6   5

CONTENTS

Unveiling a Mystery—
A Bible Study You Can Do!

UNVEILING A MYSTERY—
A BIBLE STUDY YOU CAN DO!

Hey! Are you ready to unveil a great mystery—one that a lot of grown-ups are afraid to try to uncover? Great! Then climb up in the tree house with Molly, Sam (the great detective beagle), and me. My name is Max. WHAT is this great mystery adventure? We are going to help The Discovery Bible Museum create and try out exciting, interactive, hands-on exhibits for the new Revelation wing in the museum so that kids everywhere will be able to understand the Book of Revelation.

Revelation is a very exciting book in the Bible that a lot of people think is too hard and scary to understand. But we know from 2 Timothy 3:16-17 that *"all* Scripture is inspired by God and profitable for teaching, for reproof, for correction, for training in righteousness; that the man of God may be adequate, equipped for every good work." That includes the Book of Revelation.

God put the Book of Revelation in the Bible because it tells us the rest of His story. Did you know that Revelation is the only book in the Bible that promises a blessing? Pretty cool, huh? You'll also discover WHAT happens in the future and HOW it happens. Revelation reveals WHO is in control. There's even a mysterious, sealed up book! Revelation is an *awesome* book packed with fascinating creatures and exciting events!

You can uncover the mystery of what's going to happen by studying God's Word, the Bible, the source of all truth, and by asking God's Spirit to lead and guide you. You also have this book, which is an inductive

THINGS YOU'LL NEED

NEW AMERICAN STANDARD BIBLE (UPDATED EDITION)—PREFERABLY THE NEW INDUCTIVE STUDY BIBLE (NISB)

PEN OR PENCIL   A DICTIONARY

COLORED PENCILS   THIS WORKBOOK

INDEX CARDS

Bible study. That word *inductive* means you go straight to the Bible *yourself* to investigate what the Book of Revelation shows us about Jesus Christ and the things that must soon take place. In inductive Bible study, you discover for yourself what the Bible says and means.

Doesn't that sound like fun? Grab those art supplies and stir up your imagination as we create and experiment with some very cool exhibits to help kids uncover the Bible's biggest mystery!

1

UNVEILING A MYSTERY

REVELATION 1

It's great to have you back at the tree house! Molly and I are soooo excited about this new mystery adventure! Our Uncle Jake, the archaeologist that we helped dig up truth in the Book of Genesis, works with The Discovery Bible Museum on some of his different adventures. When the museum told him about their new wing, Uncle Jake asked if we could help them create and try out the awesome exhibits.

But before we can help out, we need to do research on the Book of Revelation. Have you ever read the Book of Revelation? Being inductive Bible detectives, we know there is only one way to do our research, and that's to go straight to the main source: the Bible, God's Word. So before we head to the museum to meet Uncle Jake and Miss Kim, the museum teacher, we need to get started by searching God's Word.

UNCOVERING THE FIRST MYSTERY

Are you ready to begin your research? WHAT is the first thing you need to do? Do you remember? Pray! Way to go!

Bible study should always begin with prayer. We need to ask God to help us understand this great mystery of what is going to happen in the future and to lead and direct us by His Holy Spirit. Then we can understand what God says and make sure we handle His Word accurately.

The Book of Revelation reveals how God and Jesus triumph over Satan and evil. Because Satan doesn't want us to know the truth, he will try to discourage us and keep us from studying God's Word. So not only do we need to pray, we also need to make sure we have our armor on so we can stand firm against our enemy now and be prepared for the war against the Lamb (Revelation 17:14). We need to be strong in the Lord and in the strength of His might. Read Ephesians 6:10-17 to help you remember what your armor is.

All right, mighty warriors! Let's pray and put our armor on. Now we are ready to get started. Turn to Revelation 1 on page 141. These are our Observation Worksheets. Observation Worksheets are pages that have the Bible text printed out for you to use as you do your study on the Book of Revelation. Let's read Revelation 1:1-3.

Let's find out WHO gave the Book of Revelation, to WHOM it was given, and WHAT the revelation is. Read the first part of Revelation 1:1 again. Then fill in the blanks of the diagram on the next page and answer the questions to solve this first mystery.

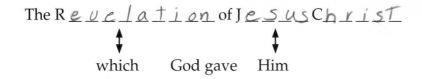

The R e v e l a t i o n of J e s u s C h r i s t

↕   ↕

which   God gave   Him

to show His bond-servants

↕

the things which must soon take place.

WHO gave the revelation? G o d

WHAT does the word *revelation* mean? Do you know? The New Testament, where the Book of Revelation is found, was originally written in Koine Greek. The Greek word for revelation is *apokalupsis*, which is pronounced like this: ap-ok-al'-oop-sis. It means "an unveiling."

Do you remember how Toto in the movie *The Wizard of Oz* pulled back the curtain and unveiled the wizard as a small man standing on a stool instead of the giant, powerful wizard Dorothy and her friends were expecting? Just like the real wizard in the movie was unveiled and they saw him as he really was, God is going to unveil what this Book of Revelation is about.

Looking back at the diagram, to WHOM did God give the revelation (the unveiling)? J e s u s

WHO is going to get the revelation? To WHOM is God going to show something?
H i s b o n d - s e r v a n t s

WHAT is God revealing? WHAT is God going to show the bond-servants? Go back to the diagram and <u>underline in red</u> WHAT God is going to show His bond-servants.

Wow! God is going to show His bond-servants what is going to happen in the future. Isn't that awesome?

Now look back at Revelation 1:1 on page 141 and get

the complete picture by filling in the details in the diagram below that shows HOW God gave the revelation to His bond-servants.

G o d

↕

gave it (the revelation) to J e s u s

↕

who communicated it by His a n g e l

↕

to His bond-servant J o h n

↕

to show to His B o n d-s e r v a n t s

WHAT is going to be shown?

The _t h i n g s_ which must _s o o n take place_.

Way to go! You have uncovered your first mystery. You have discovered WHO gives the revelation, to WHOM He gives it, and HOW He gives it. And you know WHAT the revelation is: You are going to study the things that will take place in the future. You know the revelation is true because WHO is giving it? That's right. It's coming from God.

Let's sketch what we just discovered to show Miss Kim, our museum teacher. Because museums are places of learning, there are classes, workshops, and tours to teach people about what is in the museum and why it's there. The museum teacher is in charge of all the educational programs at the museum, so Miss Kim will be the one who helps us create and experiment with the exhibits at The Discovery Bible Museum.

Draw a picture in the box on the next page to show how we got the Book of Revelation. Make sure your drawing shows what you discovered in your diagram. Show God giving the revelation to Jesus, Jesus communicating the revelation to His angel, to give to His bond-servant John, to show His bond-servants the things that must soon take place.

You can use symbols if you would like. Draw a triangle to represent God, a cross for Jesus, an angel or wings for the angel, a stick man for John, and several stick people for the bond-servants.

Great artwork! Did you know that God has a special blessing for you when you study the Book of Revelation? Let's unveil this week's memory verse to see what God has to say about this blessing. Look at the clouds below. Inside each cloud is a word from this week's verse that has been mixed up. Unscramble each word in the clouds and place it on the correct blank below the clouds.

After you have unscrambled your verse, look at Revelation 1 and find the reference for this verse. Then hide this verse in your heart by saying it aloud three times in a row three times every day.

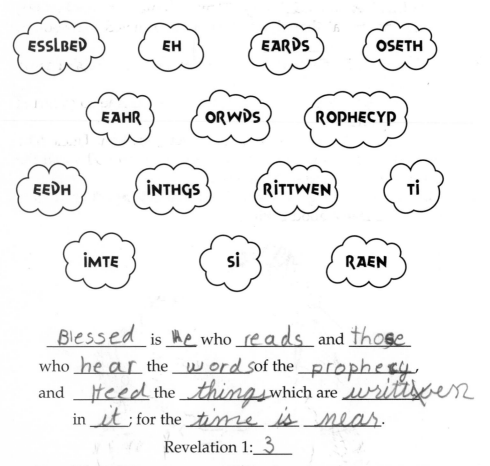

Blessed is he who reads and those who hear the words of the prophecy, and heed the things which are written in it; for the time is near.

Revelation 1: 3

You did it! Tomorrow we will head to the museum to meet Miss Kim and show her our sketches.

THE MYSTERY—HOW DO YOU RECEIVE THE BLESSING?

"Hey, guys! Over here!" Uncle Jake called as we walked into the museum. "This is the entrance to the Revelation wing, where we will discover God's plan for the future. Isn't it awesome?"

"Wow!" exclaimed Molly. "This is amazing! Look, Max, there's the mural that shows how John received the Book of Revelation."

"I can't believe how huge it is," Max replied. "I wish I could paint like that!"

"Me, too, buddy," answered Uncle Jake. "Come on over and meet Miss Kim."

"Hi, guys. It's so nice to finally meet you. Your Uncle Jake has told me all about your Bible adventures and all about the amazing Sam," laughed Miss Kim.

Sam, recognizing his name, barked and jumped up to give Miss Kim's face a good licking.

"Whoa, boy! Better get down before Miss Kim bans you from this adventure," Max said as he pulled on Sam's leash. Everyone laughed as the kids handed Miss Kim the sketches they did at the tree house to show how God gave John the Book of Revelation.

"Great job! I love your artwork! We'll put these on our kids' art wall. Do you see the area right over there with the tables and chairs? Kids who visit the museum will be able to sit there and use the art supplies to create their own sketches. Then we'll hang them on this special wall over here. What do you think about that?"

"That is soooo cool!" Max replied.

"Are you excited about what you have learned so far?" Miss Kim asked as she led the kids down the hall.

"Yes, it's awesome!" cried Molly. "We know why Revelation was written, and we can't wait to find out what's going to happen in the future."

Miss Kim smiled at Molly as she led Max, Molly, Uncle Jake, and Sam inside one of the resource rooms. "This is one of the rooms kids will work in as they learn about Revelation. Today you will work in here as you continue your research on Revelation 1."

"All right! Let's get started," Max said. "What's the first thing we need to do?"

"Pray," responded Molly.

She's right! Okay, Bible detectives. Don't forget to pray.

Yesterday as you unveiled your memory verse, you saw that someone is going to be blessed. Do you know WHO? Let's find out. Turn to page 141, and read Revelation 1:1-3 again.

Revelation is the only book in the Bible that promises a special blessing. WHO receives this blessing, and HOW do they receive it? Look at Revelation 1:3. WHO is blessed?

He who ___reads___ and those who ___hear___
___the words of the___ and ___heed___
the ___things wich are written in it.___
___prophecy___

Do you know what a prophecy is? A prophecy is when God reveals to us what is going to happen in the future. Do you see why it is so important to study this book of the Bible? But we're not just studying it. WHAT do we have to do?

We read it. We hear it. And we h _e_ _e_ _d_ it.

WHAT does it mean to heed? The word *heed* means we pay close attention to the words and keep watch. It means we don't just read and hear the words. We also pay close attention to what God is saying, and then we do it. "To heed" means to do. Are you doing what God says? *I'm trying*

Think about the things you do every day. HOW do they line up with what God says? For an example, do you pay close attention to what you look at on the Internet? Does what you look at measure up to what God says is okay, or do you look at things the world says is okay but would not please God?

Write out what kind of things you look at on the Internet on the lines below and tell if they would please God.

Bible pictures / The loch ness monster?,

Do you have time to get on the Internet and talk to your friends, but you don't have time to read the Bible and talk to God?

no

WHAT do you think God thinks about that?

its good

WHAT do you need to do? Is there anything you need to change? Write out any changes you need to make on the lines below.

ask mom before anything looking at

Great! Now that you have discovered how to receive God's blessing, let's turn back to Revelation 1 on page 141 and see what else we can discover today.

Read Revelation 1:4-8.

Revelation 1:4 To WHOM is John writing?

The _seven_ _churches_

The letters to the seven churches are not only to the seven churches in Asia but also to the bond-servants.

Read Revelation 1:4-5 again and underline in blue the first three times the word _from_ appears in these verses to find out from whom John is receiving this message.

Now, fill in the blanks.

John to the seven churches...Grace to you and peace,

from (verse 4) Him who _is_ and who _was_ and who is to _come_

WHOM are these words describing? Here's a hint: _GOD_

from (verse 4) The _seven spirits_ before His throne. (This is the Holy Spirit.)

from (verse 5a) _Jesus Christ_

Now that we have discovered WHOM this is from, let's see WHAT we can learn about God. Read Revelation 1:4 and Revelation 1:8 and list in the box on the next page HOW God is described in these two verses.

WHAT I LEARNED ABOUT GOD
He's the alpha & Omega
He's the almighty
He's on a throne

Isn't God amazing? Do you know what the words *alpha* and *omega* mean? The word *alpha*, A, is the first letter in the Greek alphabet and *omega*, Ω, is the last letter in the Greek alphabet. By calling Himself the Alpha and the Omega, God is showing us that He is the first and the last. Wow!

Now let's see what we can discover about Jesus. Read Revelation 1:5 and Revelation 1:7. WHAT are the big things you see about Jesus? List HOW Jesus is described in these two verses in the box below.

WHAT i LEARNED ABOUT jESUS

① He's the faithful witness,
② the firstborn of the dead ③
the ruler of the Kings ④ He
loved us, released us from
sin, ⑤
HE'S COMING

That's a pretty awesome description, isn't it? Did you know that Jesus is coming with the clouds? Just wait. We'll discover more about His coming as we continue our study. It's going to be quite an adventure!

All right! You have uncovered quite a few mysteries today. You have gotten a glimpse of how awesome God and Jesus are, you know Jesus is coming with the clouds and everyone will see Him, and you know how to receive a blessing. As you head out, don't forget to practice saying your memory verse (Revelation 1:3) to remind you of this special blessing.

THE MYSTERY: WHERE IS JOHN?

Hey, guys! It's great to have you back at the museum. You did a fantastic job yesterday as you discovered some awesome things about God and Jesus. Today let's find out WHAT we can discover about John. WHERE is he, WHY is he there, and WHAT is he told to do? There's only one way to find out, and that's to head back to Revelation 1. Don't forget to pray!

Now turn to page 142 and read Revelation 1:9-11. Uncover the mystery of WHERE John is and WHAT he is doing by asking the 5 W's and an H questions. What are the 5 W's and an H? They are the WHO, WHAT, WHERE, WHEN, WHY, and HOW questions.

1. Asking WHO helps you find out:
   WHO wrote this?
   WHOM are we reading about?
   To WHOM was it written?
   WHO said this or did that?

2. WHAT helps you understand:
   WHAT is the author talking about?
   WHAT are the main things that happen?

3. WHERE helps you learn:
   WHERE did something happen?
   WHERE did they go?
   WHERE was this said? When we discover a WHERE, we double underline the WHERE in green.

4. WHEN tells us about time. We mark it with a green clock or a green circle like this: ○.

WHEN tells us:
WHEN did this event happen or WHEN will it happen?
WHEN did the main characters do something? It helps
us to follow the order of events.

5. WHY asks questions like:
WHY did he say that?
WHY did this happen?
WHY did they go there?

6. HOW lets you figure out things like:
HOW is something to be done?
HOW do people know something happened?

Now ask the 5 W's and an H of Revelation 1:9-11.

Revelation 1:9 WHERE was John?

<u>*Patmos*</u>

Did you know that John was banished to this island? That
means he was sent to the island. He was not there of his own
free will. Do you know WHY he was banished here? Read
Revelation 1:9.

WHY was John on the island of Patmos?

Because of the ___*word*___ of ___*God*___ and the

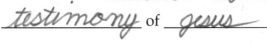

___*testimony*___ of ___*jesus*___

WHAT does that mean? John was sent to or exiled to
the barren island of Patmos because of what he testified. A

testimony is a witness—someone who tells the truth about a person's character, about who he is. John was a witness. He told the truth about Jesus. Because he would not compromise what he believed about Jesus, he was sent away. John was exiled because of his faith in Jesus.

Do you believe the truth about Jesus? If someone told you he or she believed that Jesus died to save us but that He really wasn't God, WHAT would you do? Would you be a witness for Jesus and tell the truth that Jesus was and is God, even if it meant you would be made fun of and left out of your group of friends? Or would you compromise your beliefs by not saying anything or by changing the way you think?

Write out WHAT you would do.

I would try to stand for the Lord.

Look at Revelation 1:9. WHAT was John a fellow partaker in?

in suffering with other believers

WHAT does this mean? John is suffering for what he believes. He is going through tribulations (great distress) and persevering (enduring) in Jesus for his faith. Did you know that according to tradition John was dropped in a pot of hot oil? Even though John was persecuted by being put in a pot of hot oil, he remained steadfast (firm) in Jesus' love.

Do you have faith like John? Are you willing to suffer for knowing Jesus? *yes*

Read Revelation 1:10. WHAT did John hear, and WHAT did it sound like? _a loud voice_ _that sounded like a trumpet_

Revelation 1:11 WHAT did the loud voice tell John to do? _"Write in a book what you see and send them to the 7 churches_

Name these seven churches.

1) _Ephesus_   2) _Smyrna_
3) _Pergamum_   4) _Thyatira_
5) _Sardis_   6) _Philadelphia_
7) _Laodicea_

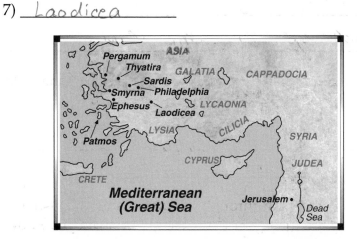

Go back and look at Revelation 1:4. WHERE are these seven churches? _in Asia_

Did you know that the Roman province of Asia is located in what we know today as Turkey? Pretty cool, huh?

You did a fantastic job today! Now, before you head out, don't forget to practice saying your memory verse. Tomorrow you will discover more of what John sees in Revelation 1:12-18.

THE MYSTERY: ONE LiKE A SON OF MAN

Hey, guys, come on in. Are you ready to do some more research? Today we are going to work in the resource room to discover what John sees. Yesterday in Revelation 1:10 we saw that John heard a loud voice that told him to write in a book what he sees. WHOSE voice was it? And WHAT can we learn about Him? Let's find out. Don't forget to pray first. Now turn to page 142 and read Revelation 1:12-18. Now ask the 5 W's and an H.

Revelation 1:12 WHAT did John see?

seven golden lampstands

Revelation 1:13 WHOM did John see?

the Son of man

WHERE was He standing?

in the middle of the lampstands

WHAT is He wearing?

a robe

Revelation 1:14 WHAT does His hair look like?

was white

WHAT are His eyes like?

a flame of fire

Revelation 1:15 WHAT do you see about His feet?

burnished bronze

WHAT was His voice like?

the sound of many waters

Revelation 1:16 WHAT is in His right hand?

7 stars

WHAT comes out of His mouth?

a two-edged sword

WHAT is His face like?

sun

Draw a picture of what this son of man looks like in the box below.

Tomorrow we will discover just WHO this son of man is. Do you know? Write out WHO you think this is on the line below.

Lord Jesus

Way to go! Now don't forget to practice saying your memory verse so that you will remember that blessed is he who reads, hears, and heeds the words of the prophecy.

DAY FIVE

THE MYSTERY OF SEVEN STARS AND SEVEN LAMPSTANDS

It's great to have you back at the museum! Miss Kim has us all set up to work in the resource room again today as we finish our research on Revelation 1. It has been an awesome week of discovery, and we are just getting started!

Are you ready to discover WHO the son of man is that John saw standing in the middle of the seven golden lampstands? And WHAT are those lampstands? Do you know? We'll find out as we pray and head back to Revelation 1.

Did you pray? Good. Now read Revelation 1:12-20 on page 142.

Do you know WHO this son of man is? Here's a clue: Verse 18 tells us He was dead and is alive forevermore. WHO died and rose again to live forever? *Lord Jesus*

Wow! What an *awesome* description of Jesus! List HOW Jesus is described in verses 17-18 in the box.

WHAT i LEARNED ABOUT JESUS

1 first and last
2 living one
3 was dead
4 will be alive forever more
5 has the keys of death & Hades

Look at Revelation 1:17 to see HOW John reacted when he saw Jesus like this. WHAT did John do?

he fell at his feet like he was dead

Now head back down the hall to see the museum mural of this awesome description of Jesus. Push the button on the wall next to the mural. WHAT do you hear?

Revelation 1:15 WHAT did John say Jesus' voice was like?

Like the sound of *many waters*

Isn't it amazing that when you push the button you can hear this awesome sound? It sounds like the roar of the waters over Niagara Falls. HOW about the next button? WHAT happens to Jesus' eyes when you push it?

Revelation 1:14 His eyes were like a *flame* of *fire*.

That's pretty amazing isn't it? Now that we know just WHO this son of man is, let's solve another mystery: WHAT do the seven stars represent, and WHAT are the seven lampstands that Jesus is standing in the middle of? Read Revelation 1:20 to uncover this mystery.

WHAT do the seven stars represent?

the angels of the 7 churches

WHAT do the seven golden lampstands represent?

the 7 churches

In Revelation 1:19, John is told to write three things. WHAT are those three things?

1. The *things* which you *have seen*
2. The *things* which *are*
3. The *things* which *will take place after* these *things*

Did you know that the Book of Revelation is written and divided into three segments by the three things that John is told to write? Let's uncover how the Book of Revelation is divided. Read Revelation 1:2, 11, and 19. Color the words see and saw blue in each of these verses.

WHAT do you think Revelation 1 is about?

The things which you have *seen*

That's what you have been studying this week—the things John saw. Look at the second thing John is told to write.

The things which *are* (Revelation 1:19).

Turn to page 143 and read the following verses in Revelation 2–3. Read Revelation 2:1, 2:8, 2:12, 2:18, 3:1, 3:7, and 3:14.

To WHOM is John told to write in these seven verses?

Revelation 1:4   The seven _chuchs_ of Asia, which are:

Revelation 2:1   E p h e s u s

Revelation 2:8   S m y r n a

Revelation 2:12   P e r g a m u m

Revelation 2:18   T h y a t i r a

Revelation 3:1   S a r d i s

Revelation 3:7   P h i l a d e l p h i a

Revelation 3:14   L a o d i c e a

Messages to these seven churches in Asia are the second thing that John is told to write. The things that *are*. These seven churches exist at the time John is given the revelation, and they are very important.

Jesus has some very specific things to say to these seven churches about how the people are living and whether they are true believers. We'll learn more about these seven churches next week.

Now turn to page 151 to uncover the third part of Revelation. Read Revelation 4:1.

WHAT are the first three words in this verse?

After   these   things

After WHAT things? WHAT did we discover Revelation 2–3 is about?

The things which ___ _are_ ___, which are the seven churches.

So WHAT do you think Revelation 4–22 will be about? Look at Revelation 1:19.

The ___ _things_ ___ which will ___ _take_ ___ _place_ ___ after _these   things_

Revelation 4–22 will be focusing on the things that happen after the seven churches. They are the things that have not happened yet. Isn't it exciting to know you are going to solve the mystery of what is going to happen in the future? But before you do, let's review all the things you have discovered this week in Revelation 1.

HOW is the Book of Revelation divided up?

Revelation 1 is about the things _____.

Revelation ____–____ is about the things _____,

which are the seven _____

Revelation ____–____ is about the things _____

_____

One more time just for practice, review WHO gave the book, HOW they received it, and WHAT it is about.

WHO? _~~angel~~ *God*_ gave the book (the revelation)

to J *e s u s*

who communicated it by His a *ngel*

to His bond-servant J *ohn*

to show His *bong-servants*

WHAT?

The *thing* which must *soon take place*

Way to go! You have uncovered some very important truths this week.

Now don't forget to say your memory verse one more time. Why don't you say it to a friend or an adult, and ask if he or she has read the words of the prophecy?

Keep up the good work! See you next week.

2

JESUS' MESSAGES TO THE CHURCHES

REVELATION 2

You're doing a fantastic job researching the Book of Revelation! Just look at what you have uncovered in just one week: You saw HOW John received the Book of Revelation, WHAT the book is about, some pretty awesome things about God and Jesus, and HOW to receive a blessing.

What do you think about the museum so far? Pretty amazing isn't it! Just wait! There is so much more to see and do as you uncover each chapter of Revelation. Are you ready to head back to the resource room and discover the mysteries of Revelation 2?

DAY ONE

YOUR FIRST LOVE

"Hey, Molly, are you ready to start uncovering the second thing John is told to write about—the things that are?"

"I sure am, Max," Molly responded. "These messages to the churches must be very important. I can't wait to see what God wants us to learn by studying those seven churches in Asia."

"Me, too! Let's pray so we can get started uncovering clues for Revelation 2."

Now that we've prayed, Bible detectives, let's look for clues in Revelation 2 to discover Jesus' message to the first church. One way you can uncover clues is by looking for key words.

What are *key words?* Key words pop up more than once. They are called key words because they help unlock the meaning of the chapter or book that you are studying and give you clues about what is most important in a passage of Scripture.

- Key words are usually used over and over again.

- Key words are important.

- Key words are used by the writer for a reason.

Once you discover a key word, you need to mark it in a special way, using a special color or symbol, so that you can immediately spot it in the Scripture. This will help you understand what you're studying. Don't forget to mark any pronouns that go with the key words, too! WHAT are pronouns? Check out Max and Molly's research card below.

Pronouns

Pronouns are words that take the place of nouns. A noun is a person, place or thing. A pronoun stands in for a noun! Here's an example: "Molly and Max are excited about their new Bible adventure. They can't wait to uncover the mysteries of Revelation!" The word *they* is a pronoun because it takes the place of Molly and Max's name in the second sentence. It is another word we use to refer to Molly and Max.

**Watch for these other pronouns
when you are marking people:**

I	you	he	she
me	yours	him	her
mine	his	hers	
we	it		
our	its		
they	them		

To discover the main people and events of Revelation 2, you need to mark the following key words on your Observation Worksheets at the back of this book.

You'll also want to make a bookmark for your key words so that you can see them at a glance as you mark them on your Observation Worksheets. Make your key word bookmark by taking an index card and writing the key words we'll show you as well as how you are going to mark them on your Observation Worksheets.

Then turn to page 143. Read Revelation 2:1-7 and mark your key words and key phrases on your Observation Worksheet. A key phrase is like a key word except it is a group of words that are repeated instead of just one word such as "I did it," "I did it," "I did it." The group of words "I did it" is a phrase that is repeated instead of just one word.

Mark the key words and key phrases on your bookmark and your Observation Worksheets. And don't forget to mark the pronouns!

To the angel of the church in (Ephesus, etc.) write (color orange)

Jesus (or any description that refers to Jesus like *The One*) (draw a purple cross and color it yellow)

I know (underline in red and color it yellow)

deeds (draw and color green feet)

love (draw and color a red heart)

repent (draw a red arrow and color the word yellow)

He who has an ear, let him hear what the spirit says to the churches (color it blue)

To him who overcomes (or He who overcomes) (color it yellow)

Don't forget to mark anything that tells you WHERE by double underlining the WHERE in green.

Now, read Revelation 2:1.

Revelation 2:1 WHO is the first church John is writing to?

_____ Ephesus _____

Before you uncover what John writes to the church in Ephesus, let's get a little background on this ancient city in Asia. Why don't we take our books and walk out into the museum to take a look at the exhibit on the seven churches?

The Roman province of Asia is located today in what we know as Turkey. As we look at the seven models of the churches in Asia (modern-day Turkey), WHAT does the museum's plaque tell us about the city of Ephesus?

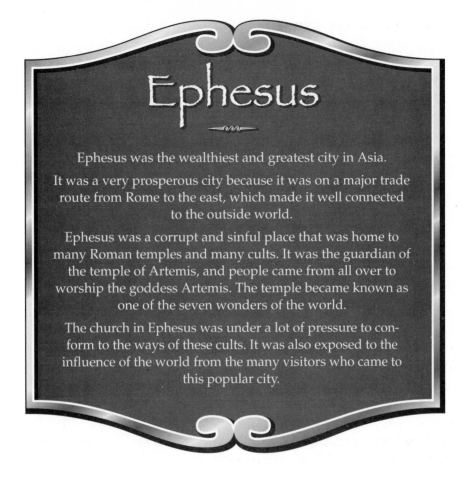

Ephesus

Ephesus was the wealthiest and greatest city in Asia.

It was a very prosperous city because it was on a major trade route from Rome to the east, which made it well connected to the outside world.

Ephesus was a corrupt and sinful place that was home to many Roman temples and many cults. It was the guardian of the temple of Artemis, and people came from all over to worship the goddess Artemis. The temple became known as one of the seven wonders of the world.

The church in Ephesus was under a lot of pressure to conform to the ways of these cults. It was also exposed to the influence of the world from the many visitors who came to this popular city.

Take a look at the large map on the wall behind the churches.

Do you see Ephesus? Great! Let's find out what we can learn about the church in Ephesus. Read Revelation 2:1-7 on page 143.

WHAT does Jesus say to the church in Ephesus? Find out by filling in the chart on the next page. Start by working on the section called "Description of Jesus."

Next, using these same verses (Revelation 2:1-7), fill in the section of the chart that says "Commendation to the Church." A commendation is when someone praises you for something you did that was good. Look at the good things Jesus says about the church in Ephesus and add those to the chart.

Now look at the section that says "Reproof Given to the Church." To reprove someone is to tell them what they are doing wrong. Fill in the chart to show what the church in Ephesus was doing wrong.

Fill in the section that says "Warnings and Instructions to the Church" by writing what Jesus tells the church at Ephesus

to do and the warning that He gives them if they don't obey.

Finally, fill in the last section on your chart that says "Promise to the Overcomers." An overcomer is someone who prevails and conquers when there is conflict and opposition. WHAT does Jesus promise those who hang in there and are victorious?

JESUS' MESSAGES TO THE CHURCHES
Church at Ephesus

Description of Jesus

Revelation 2:1 The One who holds the __seven stars__ in His __right__ __hand__, the One who __walks__ __among__ the __seven golden__ __lampstands__.

Commendation to the Church (Praise)

Revelation 2:2 I know your __deeds__ and your __toil__ and __perseverance__, and that you cannot __tolerate__ __evil__ __men__ and you put to the __test__ those who call themselves __apostles__ and they are __not__, and you found them to be __false__.

Revelation 2:3 You have __perseverance__ and __have endured__ for My name's sake, and have not grown __weary__.

Revelation 2:6 You hate the __hate__ of the __nicolaitans__ which I also __hate__.

Reproof Given to the Church (What they did wrong)

Revelation 2:4 You have __lost__ your __first love__.

Warnings and Instructions to the Church

Revelation 2:5 __remember__ from where you have __fallen__, and __repent__ and __do__ the __deeds__ you did at __first__; or else I am __coming__ to you and will __remove__ your __lampstand__ out of its __place__ —unless you __repent__.

Promise to the Overcomers

Revelation 2:7 To him who overcomes, I will __grant__ to __eat__ of the __tree__ of __life__ which is in the __paradise__ of __God__.

Wow! What a message! Look at all the good things the church at Ephesus has done: They have endured and hung in there, and they did not allow false teachers in the church.

But look at what Jesus has against them. They left their first love. Jesus is essentially telling them, "I know you love Me, but you are not loving Me the way you did when you first became a Christian. I do not have first place in your heart."

HOW important is it for God to have first place in our hearts? We'll uncover that mystery tomorrow. Look back at the "Promise to the Overcomers" on your chart. He who overcomes, Jesus will grant to eat of the tree of life. Do you know what that means? That means the overcomer will be in the new heaven! HOW do we know that? Revelation 22 shows us what the new heaven will be like. In it, in the middle of the street on either side of the river, is the tree of life bearing twelve kinds of fruit. Isn't that awesome?

Why don't you get a stick from a tree out of your yard and put some different colored gumdrops on it to represent the tree of life in the new heaven to remind you that if you overcome you will be in heaven with Jesus forever!

All right! Now let's solve this week's memory verse.

Look at the maze on the next page. Find the correct path through the church, and write the words you discover on that path on the lines below. Then check your Observation Worksheet to discover the reference of your verse.

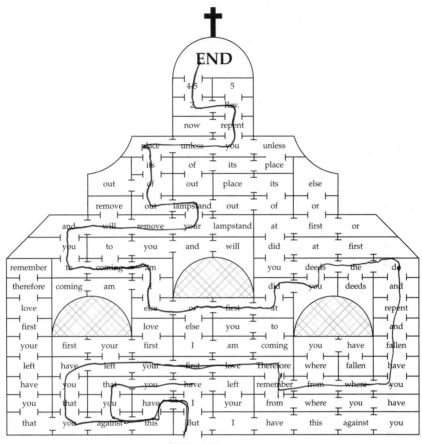

START

But I have this against you, that you have lost your first love. Therfore remember from where you have fallen, and repent and do the deeds you did at first ; or else I am coming to you and will remove your lampstand out of it's place — unless you repent.

Revelation 2: 4 - 5

Way to go! Don't forget to practice saying your verse aloud three times in a row—morning, noon, and evening today!

HOW IMPORTANT IS LOVE?

Hey! It's great to see you again. Yesterday, as we looked at the first letter John sent to the church in Ephesus, we discovered quite a bit about this church. We saw the church of Ephesus had persevered. That means the people didn't give up even though it was hard and difficult. They endured; they stood firm. And while they had not allowed false teachers in the church, they had lost their first love. They did not love God as they had in the beginning.

HOW important is it for God to have first place in our hearts? Let's find out. Don't forget to pray. Then pull out your sword of the Spirit (the Word of God, your Bible). Look up and read Mark 12:28-31. Answer the 5 W's and an H questions to solve the crossword puzzle.

Crossword puzzle with the following answers filled in:

- 17 down: love
- 19 across: property
- 3 across: love
- 18/13 across: Believes
- 5 across: GOD
- 1 across: commandment
- 14 across: hopes
- 6 across: heart
- 16 across: Fails
- 11 across: Nothing
- 8 across: mind

Mark 12:28 WHAT question does the scribe ask Jesus?

1. (Across) What __commandment__ is the
2. (Down) __foremost__ of all?

Mark 12:29-30 HOW does Jesus answer? WHAT does He say we should do in verse 30?

And you shall 3. (Across) __love__ the 4. (Down) __Lord__ your 5. (Across) __God__ with all your 6. (Across) __heart__, and with all your 7. (Down) __soul__, and with all your 8. (Across) __mind__, and with all your 9. (Down) __strength__.

Mark 12:31 WHAT is the second thing He tells them they should do?

10. (Down) You shall love your __neighbor__ as yourself.

Look up and read 1 Corinthians 13:1-13.

1 Corinthians 13:2 WHAT am I if I do not have love?

11. (Across) I am __nothing__

1 Corinthians 13:7-8 WHAT do we learn about love?

12. (Down) Love __bears__ all things, 13. (Across) __believes__ all things, 14. (Across) __hopes__ all things, 15. (Down) __endures__ all things. Love never 16. (Across) __fails__.

1 Corinthians 13:13 WHAT is the greatest of these things?

17. (Down) The greatest of these is __love__

Look up and read Acts 4:31-35.

Acts 4:32 WHAT were those who had believed doing in this verse?

Not one of them claimed that anything belonging to him was his own; but all things were 18. (Down) __common__ 19. (Across) __property__ to them.

Acts 4:34-35 Were there any needy people among these believers?

___ Yes √ No

Do you think these people had always taken care of each other and shared what they had, or do you think this happened as a result of believing in Jesus Christ?

took care of each other

Do you share your things, such as giving away a coat or shoes to someone who has a need? *somtimes*

Is this sharing with each other and giving to those in need a way to show God's love? *yes*

Wow! Jesus tells us that the greatest commandment is to love God with all our hearts, souls, minds, and strength. We also saw that we are to love our neighbors as ourselves.

If you have accepted Jesus Christ as your Savior, God is to be your first love. He is to have first place in your life. We saw from looking at 1 Corinthians 13 that love is the most important thing. Without love we are nothing! That's why we see Jesus warning the church in Ephesus about losing that first love.

HOW did Jesus tell them to fix this problem? Look back at your chart on page 35 at Revelation 2:5.

Jesus tells them to *remember* from where they have fallen. He wants them to remember how they acted when they first accepted Jesus, when He had first place in their lives.

Then He tells them to *repent* and do the *things* they did at first.

"To repent" means to change your mind about what you are doing or believing that it is wrong according to God's Word, and to decide to believe and do what God says. "To repent" is to decide to do things God's way.

Jesus is telling the people to do the things they did when they first became believers.

Did you know our actions show what we really believe? First John 3:18 tells us we are not to "love with word or with tongue, but in deed and truth." What we do shows our love.

Jesus warns the people in the church at Ephesus that if they don't do these things, He will remove their lampstand (the church) out of its place. That is pretty serious! How important is it for a church or a group of believers to love God?

as much as anything

Now that you have discovered Jesus' warning to the church in Ephesus, examine yourself.

Do you love God with all your heart, soul, mind, and strength? Is He first place in your life or have you put something else, such as friends, being popular, playing sports, or being on the Internet, in His place? Write your answer. Tell where God fits into your life. *I read the Bible morning & evening and pray whenever I can, I think God IS first place in my life*

Do you have a desire to read and study God's Word?

yes

How often do you read your Bible?

every morning & evening

Do you spend time in prayer; do you talk to God every day?

yes

Do you care about others? Do you think of them as more important than yourself? Do you put yourself or others first? *I try to put others first*

How do you treat kids at your school? Do you make fun and tease anyone? Do you try to be a friend to a kid who doesn't have a friend? Write out what you do and tell if this shows that you have God's love in you.

I try to make friends with kids that don't have friends, I think that shows god I love him

How do you show your love for God?

I try to read, uderstand, and (do) what the Bible says.

_____

_____

If, after examining yourself, you see you have left your first love, then do what Jesus told the church at Ephesus to do—

r _e p e m b e r_ from where you have fallen,
  e m e m
r _e p e n t_ (confess your sin and change your actions), and d _o_ the d _e e d s_ you did at first!

Remember, he who overcomes, Jesus will grant to eat of the tree of life! Way to go! You've finished Day Two. We are so proud of you!

DAY THREE

BE FAITHFUL—STAND FIRM

"Hold on, Sam! We're in the museum; take it easy!" Max called out as Sam raced down the hallway. Sam had spotted Miss Kim standing by the models of the churches, and he wanted to be the first to greet her with a good face lick!

Miss Kim looked up in astonishment and smiled as she watched Sam drag Max down the hallway. But her smile started to fade as she realized Sam was making a beeline in her direction. Molly came panting from behind. "Watch out, Miss Kim! Stand firm 'cause here comes Sam!"

Miss Kim braced herself as Sam slid up to her feet and jumped with all his might to lick her face.

"Down, boy," she said. "I missed you, too!

"Come on, cool it, we have to get back to work to find out what Jesus had to say to the second church in Asia," Max said. Sam sighed and then sat down and wagged his tail. He was ready to get to work. How about you? Are you ready to discover what Jesus has to say to the next church?

Don't forget to pray! Now pull out your key word bookmark and add the new key words listed to your index card.

Satan (devil) (draw a red pitchfork)

second death (underline twice in black)

Turn to page 144. Read Revelation 2:8-11 and mark your two new key words and the key words listed below on your Observation Worksheet just like they are on your index card. Turn to page 139 if you have lost your card. Don't forget to mark the pronouns!

To the angel of the church in Smyrna write

Jesus (or any description that refers to Jesus)

I know

He who has an ear, let him hear what the spirit says to the churches

To him who overcomes (or He who overcomes)

Don't forget to mark anything that tells you <u>WHERE</u> by double underlining the <u>WHERE</u> in green. And don't forget to mark anything that tells you WHEN by drawing a green clock or green circle like this: .

Revelation 2:8 WHAT church is this message for? _____

Smyrna

WHAT does the museum's plaque tell us about the city of Smyrna?

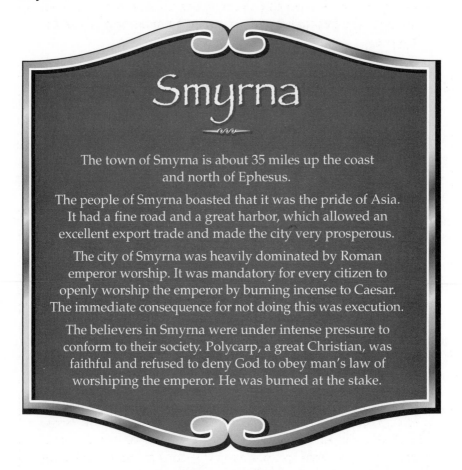

Smyrna

The town of Smyrna is about 35 miles up the coast and north of Ephesus.

The people of Smyrna boasted that it was the pride of Asia. It had a fine road and a great harbor, which allowed an excellent export trade and made the city very prosperous.

The city of Smyrna was heavily dominated by Roman emperor worship. It was mandatory for every citizen to openly worship the emperor by burning incense to Caesar. The immediate consequence for not doing this was execution.

The believers in Smyrna were under intense pressure to conform to their society. Polycarp, a great Christian, was faithful and refused to deny God to obey man's law of worshiping the emperor. He was burned at the stake.

Polycarp was a martyr for his faith. A martyr is someone who chooses to die rather than give up what he or she believes in. It is someone who dies for his or her faith. If you want to learn more about Christians who died for their faith, you can read *Foxe's Christian Martyrs of the World*. Take a look on the next page at what Max and Molly discovered about Polycarp.

Polycarp

Polycarpus (also known as Polycarp) was a follower and convert of St. John the Evangelist and served in the ministry of Christ for 60 years.

Polycarp was martyred in his eighty-sixth year.

When Polycarp discovered he was in danger of being killed because he was Christian, he escaped; but a child discovered his hiding place. Then he had a dream of his bed suddenly becoming on fire. Because of these two circumstances, Polycarp thought that it was God's will that he should suffer martyrdom, so he did not try to escape the next time he had a chance.

When Polycarp was taken before the proconsul he was cheerful and serene. He asked for one hour of prayer and was led to the marketplace to be burned alive. Polycarp prayed earnestly to heaven. As the fire and flames grew hot, the executioners had to move away because the heat of the fire was too hot for them to stand near.

Even though the fire was so intense, the fire did not consume Polycarp's body. Polycarp sang praises to God in the middle of the flames while the burning of the wood spread a fragrance around. Astonished at the miracle but determined to put an end to Polycarp's life, the guards stuck spears into his body. There was so much blood that it put out the fire. It took many, many times for them to finally put Polycarp to death, but once he was dead they were finally able to burn his body.[1]

---

1. John Foxe and other eminent authorities, *Foxe's Christian Martyrs of the World* (Chicago: Moody Press), pp. 55-56.

Wow! Are you amazed at how much Polycarp loved Jesus? Look at how he praised God even when he was being burned alive!

Now, let's find out more about the church at Smyrna.

Take a look at the large map on the wall behind the churches. Can you find the city of Smyrna? Great! Now look back at Revelation 2:8-11 and fill in the chart on the next page to show what Jesus says to the church in Smyrna. The first thing you need to fill in is the section that describes Jesus.

Next, from these same verses, fill in the section of the chart that says "Commendation to the Church." Remember a commendation is when someone praises you for something you did that was good. Look at the good things Jesus says about the church in Smyrna, and add those to your chart.

Look at Revelation 2:8-11. Is there any *reproof* (correction) given to the church at Smyrna?

<u>_____ *no* _____</u>

Now, fill in the section that says "Warnings and Instructions to the Church." What is Jesus warning the church at Smyrna about? What should they do?

Fill in the last section on your chart that says "Promise to the Overcomers." WHAT does Jesus promise those who hang in there and are victorious?

JESUS' MESSAGES TO THE CHURCHES

Church at Smyrna

Description of Jesus

Revelation 2:8 The __first__ and the __last__, who was __dead__, and has come to __life__.

Commendation to the Church (Praise)

Revelation 2:9 I know your __tribulation__ and your __poverty__ (but you are __rich__), and the __blasphemy__ by those who say they are __Jews__ and are not, but are a __synagogue__ of __Satan__.

Reproof Given to the Church

Does Jesus point out anything they are doing wrong? __no__

Warnings and Instructions to the Church

Revelation 2:10 Do not __fear__ what you are about to __suffer__. Behold, the __devil__ is about to __cast__ some of you into __prison__, so that you will be __tested__, and you will have __tribulation__ for __ten__ days. Be __faithful__ until __death__, and I will give you the __crown__ of __life__.

Promise to the Overcomers

Revelation 2:11 He who __overcomes__ will not be __hurt__ by the __second__ __death__.

Isn't this awesome? Jesus doesn't have any reproof for the church at Smyrna. Was it a perfect church? Why do you think Jesus didn't have any correction for this church?

Because they were a good church

While we saw that Ephesus was a church that lost its first love, Smyrna could be characterized as a suffering church. They have already suffered tribulations and poverty, and now Jesus warns them they are about to be tested with more suffering. Some people will even be cast into prison and lose their lives.

Remember what we read about Polycarp? If people love Jesus so much that they are suffering for His sake, do they need reproving? Jesus doesn't need to correct this church because of the suffering it is going through. When we are willing to suffer and willing to obey, it proves the genuineness of our love for Jesus.

Look back at your chart to the description of Jesus. Why do you think Jesus describes Himself this way to the church of Smyrna? How would this description help those people who are suffering?

That they will live after they die, in heaven

Don't you think it would be a comfort knowing that death didn't have a hold on Jesus if you knew you may be put to death for your faith? Thinking of Jesus as being dead but now alive would give you hope. We do not have to fear death because Jesus conquered it when He died and rose again!

Revelation 2:10-11 WHAT does Jesus promise the people of the church at Smyrna if they remain faithful until death? I will give you _the crown of life_.

He who overcomes _will not be hurt by the second death_

WHAT does that mean? Look up and read Revelation 20:14. WHAT is the second death?

its the lake of fire

If you are an overcomer, you will not be hurt by the lake of fire! The lake of fire is only for those who don't believe in Jesus. Believers in Jesus are not thrown into the lake of fire. They are saved from eternal death. They will live with Jesus forever (Revelation 20:6,13-15)!

Now ask yourself:

Are you willing to be a Polycarp? Do you love Jesus so much that you are willing to suffer and maybe even die for Him? _I think so_

Have you ever suffered for your faith by being made fun of because you wouldn't do some of the things other kids do that you know are wrong or for saying you are a Christian? _no_

Write what happened. _____

_____

_____

Have you seen the movie or read the book *The End of the Spear?* It's about the missionaries who gave their lives to share Christ. Would you be willing to serve God on the mission field if you knew it would cost your life?

yes _____

Would you be willing to witness to someone who took the life of someone you loved? _yes_

Look up and read Matthew 5:10. WHAT are those who have been persecuted for the sake of righteousness? B l e s s e d!

Isn't this amazing! We will be blessed when we are persecuted. WHAT will we receive?

The *kingdom* of *heaven*.

Make a crown out of some poster board and either draw and color some jewels on it or glue some play jewels from the craft store on it to remind you what the overcomer gets when he or she endures suffering.

Sometimes we are afraid to stand up for what we believe in. We are afraid to say no or to go against the crowd. We don't want to suffer or be hurt so we give in and compromise what we believe.

We need to remember that when we suffer, are made fun of, or left out because of what we believe, it is only a temporary situation, and it will never be more than we are able to handle. We do not need to fear. We need to trust God and do what He says is right.

God is in control of our situation. He knows everything that is happening to us! Sometimes God allows us to go through "the fire" to purify us and test our faith (James 1:2-4). He wants us to be perfect and complete—lacking in nothing!

Jesus reminded the church at Smyrna not to be afraid but to be faithful. We need to remember that. We need to hang in there and overcome so we will be blessed and receive the crown of life!

THE SHARP, TWO-EDGED SWORD

You made an awesome discovery yesterday as you looked at Jesus' message to the suffering church of Smyrna. WHAT will we uncover today as we look at Jesus' message to the third church? Let's find out. Ask God to open your eyes to His truth, and then pull out your key word bookmark and turn to page 145.

Read Revelation 2:12-17 and mark the key words on your Observation Worksheet just like they are on your index card. Turn to page 139 if you have lost your card.

Don't forget to mark the pronouns!

To the angel of the church in Pergamum write

Jesus (or any description that refers to Jesus like *The One*)

I know   Satan   repent

He who has an ear, let him hear what the spirit says to the churches

To him who overcomes (or He who overcomes)

Don't forget to mark anything that tells you <u>WHERE</u> by double underlining the <u>WHERE</u> in green. And don't forget to mark anything that tells you WHEN by drawing a green clock or green circle like this: ○.

Read Revelation 2:12.

WHAT church is this message for? *Pergamum*

Now take a look at the next museum plaque. WHAT does it teach us about the city of Pergamum?

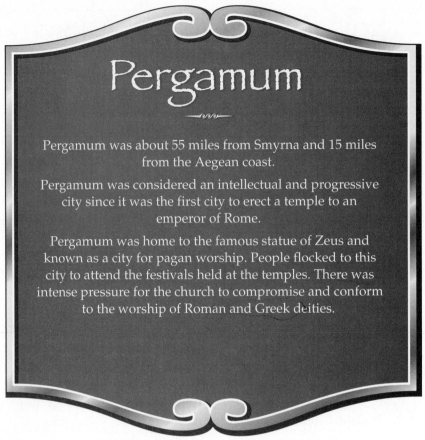

Pergamum

Pergamum was about 55 miles from Smyrna and 15 miles from the Aegean coast.

Pergamum was considered an intellectual and progressive city since it was the first city to erect a temple to an emperor of Rome.

Pergamum was home to the famous statue of Zeus and known as a city for pagan worship. People flocked to this city to attend the festivals held at the temples. There was intense pressure for the church to compromise and conform to the worship of Roman and Greek deities.

Now take a look at the map. Can you find the city of Pergamum? Way to go! Look back at Revelation 2:12-17 on page 145, and fill in the chart on the next page to show what Jesus says to the church in Pergamum.

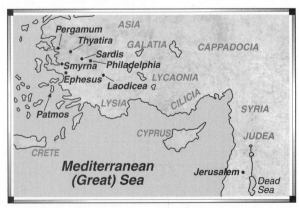

JESUS' MESSAGES TO THE CHURCHES
Church at Pergamum

Description of Jesus

Revelation 2:12 The __one__ who has the sharp __two-edged__ __sword__

Commendation to the Church (Praise)

Revelation 2:13 I know where you __dwell__ where __satans__ __throne__ is; and you __hold fast__ My __name__, and did not __deny__ My __faith__.

Reproof Given to the Church (What they did wrong)

Revelation 2:14 But I have a few things against you, because you have there some who hold the __teaching__ of __Balaam__, who kept __teaching__ Balak to put a __stumbling block__ before the sons of Israel, to __eat__ things __sacrificed__ to __idols__, and to commit acts of __immorality__.

Revelation 2:15 Some who in the same way hold the __same__ __teaching__ of the __Nicolaitans__.

Warnings and Instructions to the Church

Revelation 2:16 __Repent__; or else I am __coming__ to you __quickly__, and I will make __war__ against them with the __sword__ of My __mouth__.

Promise to the Overcomers

Revelation 2:17 [He] who overcomes, to him I will __give__ some of the __hidden__ __mana__, and I will give him a __white__ __stone__, and a __new__ __name__ written on the __stone__ which no one knows but he who __recieves__ it.

Ephesus had lost their first love; Smyrna was a suffering church. WHAT do we learn about Pergamum? Pergamum had held fast to Jesus' name and did not deny their faith, but they had also allowed wrong teaching in the church. Do you think Jesus is happy about the false teaching? Look back on your chart at Jesus' warning.

WHAT does Jesus tell them to do? R _e p e nt_ . That means to change what they are doing or else WHAT?
_____He will_____punish____them_____

_____

HOW is Jesus described on your chart? WHAT could this sword be? Let's find out by going to other passages of Scripture. When we compare Scripture with other Scripture, that's called *cross-referencing*. Always remember that *Scripture never contradicts Scripture*.

Look up and read Ephesians 6:17. WHAT is the sword of the Spirit? ___the Bible_____

Now look up and read Hebrews 4:12.

WHAT do we learn about the Word of God?
It is __living__ and __active__ and __sharper__ than any
__two__ -edged __sword__, and_____ as far as the division
of _____ and _____, of both _____ and
_____, and able to _____ the _____
and _____ of the _____.

Isn't that awesome! God's Word is sharper than any two-edged sword. It is living and active! That's why it is so very important that you learn how to study the Bible for yourself! God tells us in 2 Timothy 2:15, "Be diligent to present yourself approved to God as a workman who does not need to be ashamed, accurately handling the word of truth."

God also tells us in Titus 1:9 that we are to hold fast the faithful word so we will be able to exhort (encourage, preach) in sound doctrine (healthy teaching) and to refute (expose) those who contradict (to speak against), which in this case would be exposing those who speak against the truth.

We have to be diligent to handle God's Word accurately and be very careful not to allow false teachers in the church like they did at Pergamum.

> Are you willing to do that? Will you study God's Word so you can know the truth and expose those who aren't teaching the truth? _yes_
>
> Do you think that wrong teaching might be why so many churches are having problems today? _yes I do._

> Will you measure everything—the movies you watch, the books you read, the friends you hang out with—by God's standard and if it doesn't measure up to what God says, will you continue to do those things? Write out what you will do. _I would take 5 min. of and give them to God_

All right! Now, WHAT does the overcomer receive this time? This time we see three things: hidden manna, a white stone, and a new name.

In the Old Testament (Exodus 16:31-35), manna was the bread from heaven that God fed the children of Israel in the wilderness, and it was also put into the Ark of the Covenant (or Testimony). In the New Testament, in John 6:31-35, we see Jesus is the bread of life. Overcomers get heavenly bread—the bread of life. They also get a white stone, which was used for voting when someone was tried for a crime by a court. The jurors would cast their vote to acquit the person of the crime by laying down a white stone. Isn't that awesome? Jesus acquitted us of our sins! A white stone was also used as an admission ticket to a banquet. Do you know of a banquet that Christians will attend in heaven? How about the marriage supper of the Lamb (Revelation 19:9)?

And overcomers receive a new name on the white stone. In Bible times a person's name was very significant because it showed the person's character and attributes. Overcomers receive a new name, one that identifies them with Jesus and shows the new life they have in Him.

Why don't you get a rock and paint it white to remind you that if you overcome, you are completely and totally accepted by Jesus and forgiven of your sins. You belong to Him and have a ticket into heaven!

You have done an awesome job and learned some very important truths today about suffering for what is right and teaching truth. Keep up the good work by practicing your memory verses so the truth will be hidden in your heart! Tomorrow we will discover what God says to the next church.

DO YOU TOLERATE SIN?

It's great to have you back at the museum again! Today we are going to find out what Jesus has to say to the next church. Are you surprised by what you have uncovered about these churches? Don't forget to pray! Now let's uncover Jesus' message to the fourth church.

Pull out your key word bookmark and turn to page 146. Read Revelation 2:18-29 and mark the key words listed on your Observation Worksheet just like they are on your index card. Turn to page 139 if you have lost your card.

Don't forget to mark the pronouns!

To the angel of the church in Thyatira write

Jesus (or any description that refers to Jesus, like *Son of God*)

I know   deeds   love   repent

Satan

He who has an ear, let him hear what the spirit says to the churches

To him who overcomes (or He who overcomes)

Don't forget to mark anything that tells you WHERE by double underlining the WHERE in green. And don't forget to mark anything that tells you WHEN by drawing a green clock or green circle like this: ○ .

Read Revelation 2:18.
WHAT church is this message for? _Thyatira_

WHAT does the museum's plaque tell about the city of Thyatira?

Thyatira

The city of Thyatira was smaller than Ephesus, Smyrna, and Pergamum.

Thyatira was a city that had many skilled craftsmen who worked in trade guilds. Trade guilds were associations for bakers, bronze workers, clothiers, cobblers, etc. The power of the guilds was their ability to make the most beautiful articles and take over the market.

The craftsmen wanted to be part of these guilds since their success depended on being part of one of these groups. But some were kept out of the guilds.

Since the trade guilds profited heavily on the sale of the instruments for the temple, the people became extremely active in idol worship, which caused them to put great pressure on the church to compromise.

Take a look at the large map on the wall. Can you find the city of Thyatira? All right! Now look back on page 146 at Revelation 2:18-29 and fill in the chart below to show what Jesus says to the church in Thyatira.

JESUS' MESSAGES TO THE CHURCHES
Church at Thyatira

Description of Jesus
Revelation 2:18 The ___*son*___ of ___*God*___ who has ___*eyes*___ like a ___*flame*___ of ___*fire*___, and His ___*feet*___ are like ___*burnished-bronze*___.

Commendation to the Church (Praise)
Revelation 2:19 I know your ___*deeds*___, and your ___*love*___ and ___*faith*___ and ___*service*___ and ___*perserverance*___ and that your ___*deeds*___ of ___*late*___ are ___*greater*___ than at ___*first*___.

Reproof Given to the Church (What they did wrong)
Revelation 2:20 But I have this against you, that you ___*tolerate*___ the ___*woman Jezebel*___,

who calls herself a *prophetess* and she *teaches* and *leads* My *bond-servants astray*, so that they *commit acts* of *immorality* and *eat* things *sacrificed* to *idols*.

Warnings and Instructions to the Church

Revelation 2:21 I gave her *time* to *repent*, and she does *not want* to *repent* of her *immorality*.

Revelation 2:22 I will *throw* her on a bed of *sickness*, and those who *commit adultery* with her into *great tribulation*, *unless* they *repent* of her *deeds*.

Revelation 2:23 And I will *kill* her children with *pestilence*, and all the *churches* will know that I am He who *searches* the *minds* and *hearts*; and I will *give* to each one of you according to your *deeds*.

Revelation 2:24-25 The *rest* who are in Thyatira, who do *not* hold this *teaching*, who have not known the deep things of *Satan*, as they call them—I place *no* other *burden* on *you*. Nevertheless what you have, *hold fast until* I *come*.

Promise to the Overcomers

Revelation 2:26-28 He who overcomes, and he who *keeps* My *deeds* until the *end*, to him I will give *authority* over the *nations*; and he shall *rule* them with a *rod* of *iron*, as the vessels of the *potter* are *broken* to *pieces* as I also have received *authority* from My Father; and I will *give* him the *morning star*.

Wow! Look at the good things Jesus says to the church in Thyatira. They are loving, serving, persevering, and their deeds are greater now than they were in the beginning. They are a growing church!

So WHAT are they doing wrong? They have allowed an evil woman in the church to teach and lead others into immorality. Immorality is a sin. It means to be intimate with someone you are not married to. They are tolerating sin in the church at Thyatira.

WHAT does God's Word have to say about what we are to be as believers in Jesus and how we are to live? Are we to allow sin in our lives and our church? Let's find out. Look up and read Ephesians 1:4.

WHAT did God choose us to be before Him?

_____

Look up and read 1 Thessalonians 4:3-8.

1 Thessalonians 4:3 WHAT are we to abstain from?

_____

1 Thessalonians 4:4 WHAT are we to know how to do?

_____

1 Thessalonians 4:7 WHAT has God called us for?

_____

WHAT does this word "sanctification" mean? The Greek word for sanctification is *hagiasmos.* It is pronounced like this: hag-ee-as-mos´. It means purity, holiness. God has called us to be pure and holy.

Look up Romans 12:1-2.

Romans 12:1 HOW are we to present our bodies?

_____

Romans 12:2 WHAT are we not to be?

_____

_____

Romans 12:2 HOW are we to be transformed?

_____

That means we are not to be shaped into the world's mold. We're not to do the things the world says is okay but God tells us in His Word are wrong! We are to be different. We are to line ourselves up with what God's Word says is right.

WHAT does God say about sin in the church? Look up and read 1 Corinthians 5:7-13.

1 Corinthians 5:7 WHAT does Paul tell them to clean out?

_____

Did you know that when the Bible talks about sin it sometimes uses leaven as a picture of sin? So WHAT is Paul really telling them to clean out? _____

1 Corinthians 5:9 WHO does Paul tell them not to associate with?

_____

1 Corinthians 5:11-13 Does Paul mean all immoral people, or is he talking about those who say they are believers in Jesus but are continuing in sin inside the church?

_____

Do you see WHY Jesus is upset with the church at Thyatira? They were a loving and growing people who were tolerating sin inside the church when they knew it was wrong and should clean it out.

Now think about your life.

Have you allowed sin in your life? Are you doing things you know God says is wrong?

_____ *yes* _____

WHAT are you doing wrong?

_____ *arguing* _____

Is your mind shaped by the world or transformed by God's Word?

_____ *½* _____

WHAT kind of friends do you hang out with?

_____ *good one's* _____

Are you tolerating sin by hanging out with friends who say they are believers in Jesus but have a lifestyle of sin?

_____ *no* _____

Does the influence and pressure of your friends determine what you wear?

_____ *no* _____

WHAT kinds of clothes do you and the kids in your group wear? Do you wear T-shirts with inappropriate messages or clothes that reveal too much?

_____ *no* _____

Do you honor God with the way you dress, or do you just want to look cool and popular?

_____ *I honor God with the way I dress*

WHAT is your language and music like? Do your words and the words in your music glorify God?

_____ *yes* _____

So WHAT do you do if, after examining your heart, you discover you are like Thyatira, that you have tolerated sin in your life?

Look back at Revelation 2:22. WHAT did Jesus tell them to do?

repent of her _deeds_

Go to God and confess what you are doing wrong. Change your mind about what you're doing, and then change your actions. Ask God to forgive you and help you do what He says is right!

First John 1:9 says, "If we confess our sins, He is faithful and righteous to forgive us our sins and to cleanse us from all unrighteousness."

Now look back at your chart. What does Jesus promise the overcomer? Authority over the nations. Wow! What does that mean? Look at Revelation 5:10 and Revelation 20:6. We are going to reign with Christ!

What about the morning star Jesus will give us? Look at Revelation 22:16.

WHO is the bright morning star? J_e s u_ _ _

When you accept Jesus as your Savior, He comes into your heart and dwells with you. Isn't that awesome? We are given Jesus to be with us always!

Why don't you get a piece of cardboard and cut it out into the shape of a star. Cover it with aluminum foil to remind you, as an overcomer, Jesus will give you the morning star! You could also take an empty paper towel tube and make a scepter out of it to remind you that if you overcome you will reign with Christ!

Now don't forget to say your memory verse to a grown-up, to remind you of WHO is to be your first love. God loves you! When you sin, remember and repent. God will cleanse you from all your sins so you will be holy and blameless before Him!

3

ARE YOU AN OVERCOMER?

REVELATION 3

This week as we begin our research on Revelation 3, we will finish up Jesus' last three messages to the churches in Asia. We'll also answer the question "Are you an overcomer?" Jesus has some pretty awesome promises for those who overcome (persevere and conquer), and we need to find out just what it takes to be an overcomer.

Are you ready to continue this great adventure? Okay! Grab your "sword of truth," warrior of God, and head back to the museum.

THE MYSTERY—GENUINE OR FAKE?

Welcome back to the resource room. Shhhhh! We don't want to wake Sam. You know how he loves messing up the craft supplies in the cabinets. Today we need to start our research by observing Revelation 3:1-6 and marking our key words. Don't forget to pray!

Pull out your key word bookmark and add the two new key words to your index card.

seven Spirits (draw a purple ⌒ and color it yellow)

white garments (white robe) (color it yellow)

Turn to page 147. Read Revelation 3:1-6 and mark your new key words and the key words listed below on your Observation Worksheet just like they are on your index card. Turn to page 139 if you have lost your card.

Don't forget to mark the pronouns!

To the angel of the church in Sardis write

Jesus (or any description that refers to Jesus)

I know   deeds   repent

He who has an ear, let him hear what the spirit says to the churches

To him who overcomes (or He who overcomes)

Don't forget to mark anything that tells you <u>WHERE</u> by double underlining the <u>WHERE</u> in green. And don't forget to mark anything that tells you WHEN by drawing a green clock or green circle like this: ◯ .

Now let's find out what Jesus has to say to the fifth church in Asia. Read Revelation 3:1.

WHAT church is this message for? _Sardis_

Looking at the museum's plaque, WHAT does it tell us about this city?

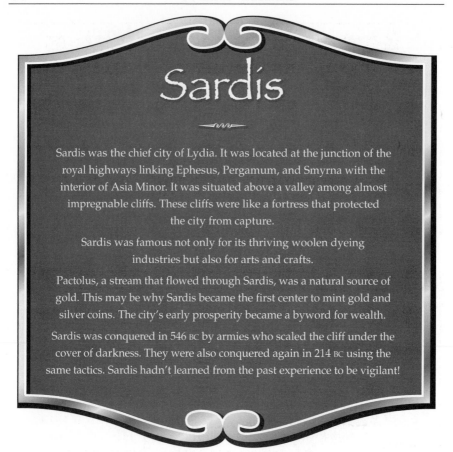

Sardis

Sardis was the chief city of Lydia. It was located at the junction of the royal highways linking Ephesus, Pergamum, and Smyrna with the interior of Asia Minor. It was situated above a valley among almost impregnable cliffs. These cliffs were like a fortress that protected the city from capture.

Sardis was famous not only for its thriving woolen dyeing industries but also for arts and crafts.

Pactolus, a stream that flowed through Sardis, was a natural source of gold. This may be why Sardis became the first center to mint gold and silver coins. The city's early prosperity became a byword for wealth.

Sardis was conquered in 546 BC by armies who scaled the cliff under the cover of darkness. They were also conquered again in 214 BC using the same tactics. Sardis hadn't learned from the past experience to be vigilant!

Take a look at the large map on the wall. Can you find the city of Sardis? Good work! Look back on page 147 at Revelation 3:1-6, and fill in the chart on the next page to show what Jesus says to the church in Sardis.

JESUS' MESSAGES TO THE CHURCHES
Church at Sardis

Description of Jesus
Revelation 3:1 He who has the _seven_ _spirits_ of God and the _seven_ _stars_.

Commendation to the Church (Praise)
Revelation 3:4 But you have a _few_ _people_ in Sardis who have not _soiled_ their _garments_, and they will _walk_ with Me in _white_, for they are _worthy_.

Reproof Given to the Church (What they did wrong)
Revelation 3:1 I know your _deeds_, that you have a _name_ that you are _alive_, but you are _dead_.

Revelation 3:2 I have not found your _deeds_ _completed_ in the sight of My God.

Warnings and Instructions to the Church
Revelation 3:2 _Wake_ _up_, and _strengthen_ the things that _remain_, which were about to _die_.

Revelation 3:3 So _remember_ what you have _recieved_ and _heard_ and _keep_ it, and _repent_. Therefore if you do not _wake up_, I will come like a _thief_, and you will not know at what _hour_ I will _come_ to you.

Promise to the Overcomers
Revelation 3:5 He who overcomes will thus be _clothed_ in _white_ _garments_; and I will not _erase_ his _name_ from the _book_ of _life_, and I will _confes_ his _name_ before My Father and before His angels.

Did you notice that only a few people in the church at Sardis received praise from Jesus?

WHAT was the good thing that these few people had done?

they didn't soile their white garments

Write WHAT you think this means.

they were pure

White symbolizes purity. Soiled means to stain or defile. These few people that had not soiled (stained) their garments were pure. They were not living a lifestyle of sin. They were following Jesus. They were true, godly believers in the church.

Look up Revelation 19:7-8.

HOW does the bride make herself ready?

_____

WHAT is the fine linen?

It is the _____ _____ of the s __ __ __ __ __.

So ask yourself: When I get dressed up, I look good on the outside, but what do I look like on the inside?

_____

If you have a relationship with Jesus then there will be some purity in your life. WHAT did we learn about the church at Sardis—WHAT was wrong with this church? Jesus said they had a reputation of being alive, but they were dead.

The church looked like a good, solid church. It was well regarded in the city and neighborhood. But while it looked alive, it was really dead! The church at Sardis had a religion but not a relationship with Jesus Christ. With the exception of a few people, they were a church in name only. Their deeds were not completed.

Look up and read Titus 1:16

WHAT did these people profess?

_____

Titus 1:16 WHAT did their deeds do?

_____

Titus 1:16 HOW are these people described?

_____

• So from what you have uncovered, do you think everyone who goes to church is a true believer in Jesus Christ?

_____

• WHAT is your reputation like? Do you have a reputation of a true believer who walks and has a relationship with God? Or are you a believer in name only—you go to church but you don't spend time with God or do the things God tells you to do in His Word?

Write out WHAT your reputation says about you and whether it is really true or not.

_____

_____

_____

Remember, you may be able to fool other people, but you cannot fool God. Jesus told the people at the church at Sardis, "I know your deeds..."

Jesus knows our hearts. He sees us for what we are, not what we may pretend to be. Read 1 Samuel 16:7: "...for God sees not as man sees, for man looks at the outward appearance, but the LORD looks at the heart."

HOW could the people at the Sardis church fix their problem? Could it be fixed?

Revelation 3:2 WHAT did Jesus say?

Wake up and strengthen the things that remain which were about

Revelation 3:3 R _emember_ what you have _recieved_ and _heard_; and _keep_ it, and _repent_ .

Those R's must be really important because Jesus uses them over and over again! Remember and repent. Jesus wants us to turn to Him and change our ways. He is a God of second chances. The reason He warns us is because He loves us and wants us to return to Him.

WHAT will happen if the church doesn't wake up? Jesus will come like a thief. That's when it will be too late to change.

Remember: God is a God of love and forgiveness, but He is also a righteous God. Because of His righteousness, He must judge sin.

As we wrap up our research today, think about what you have learned. Ask yourself, Do I really believe or am I a Christian in name only? Do I have religion or a relationship with Jesus?

All right! You did great! What does the overcomer receive? He or she is clothed in white garments—that means the overcomer's sin will be covered by Christ's righteousness. Wow! And the overcomer's name will not be erased from the book of life. Did you know that only people whose names are not written in the book of life are thrown into the lake of fire (Revelation 20:15)? If we overcome, we do not need to fear because our names will be written in the book of life and we will live forever with Jesus.

Why don't you get some construction paper and notebook paper and make a book? On the front write "The Book of Life," and inside write your name to remind yourself that if you are an overcomer, your name will not be erased from the book!

Before we wake Sam and take him outside for a treat, let's uncover your new memory verse this week by looking at the Bible below. Cross out every third letter inside the Bible, and write the letters that are left (the ones that aren't crossed out) on the blanks underneath the Bible.

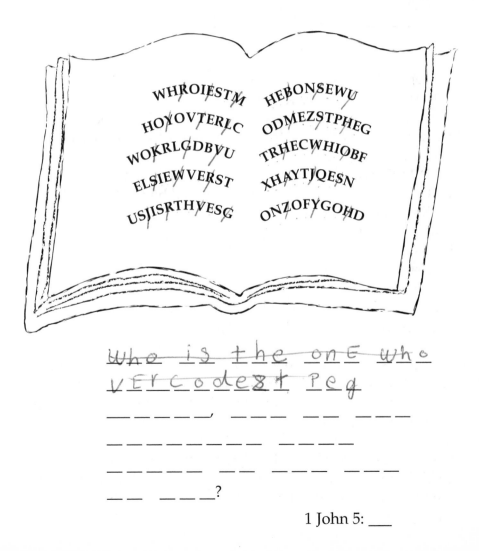

WHROIESTM   HEBONSEWU

HOYOVTERLC   ODMEZSTPHEG

WOKRLGDBVU   TRHECWHIOBF

ELSIEWVERST   XHAYTJQESN

USJISRTHVESG   ONZOFYGOHD

Who is the one who vercodest Peg

_ _ _ _ _ , _ _ _ _ _ _ _

_ _ _ _ _ _ _ _ _ _ _

_ _ _ _ _ _ _ _ _ _ _ _

_ _ _ _ _ ?

1 John 5: ___

Great work! Now look up and read 1 John 5 in your Bible until you find the reference for this verse. Fill in the reference.

Don't forget to practice saying this verse three times in a row, three times every day this week!

THE MYSTERY—A LiTTLE POWER

"Hey, Molly, isn't it cool that we get to see all the things Jesus has to say about the seven churches in Asia?" Max asked as he and Molly looked at the different models of the churches in the museum.

"It sure is. I am so amazed at how much I've learned. Look at how these models are designed to show what the churches were really like. I didn't notice it until we started doing our research. Isn't it awesome?"

"Just wait," Miss Kim said as she walked up. "After you finish your study on all seven churches, you and Max get to pick one church and design a model of it to show that church's strengths and weaknesses."

"That sounds like fun," Max replied. "Will all the kids who

visit the museum get a chance to create their own models of a church?"

"They sure will. After they finish they can either leave it here for our kids' display or they can take it home to remind them of what they've learned about Jesus and that specific church."

"I can't wait," Molly said. "Why don't we pray so we can uncover Jesus' message to the sixth church?"

Let's go, Bible detectives. Pray. Then turn to page 148. Pull out your key word bookmark and add the new key word listed to your index card.

those who dwell on the earth (color it green)

Read Revelation 3:7-13 and mark your new key word and the key words listed below on your Observation Worksheet just like they are on your index card. Turn to page 139 if you have lost your card.

Don't forget to mark the pronouns!

To the angel of the church in Philadelphia write

Jesus (or any description that refers to Jesus)

I know   deeds   love   Satan

He who has an ear, let him hear what the spirit says to the churches

To him who overcomes (or He who overcomes)

Don't forget to mark anything that tells you <u>WHERE</u> by double underlining the <u>WHERE</u> in green. And don't forget to mark anything that tells you WHEN by drawing a green clock ⏰ or green circle like this: ○.

Read Revelation 3:7.

WHAT church is this message for?

    Philadelphia

Look at the museum's plaque on the next page to see WHAT it tells us about the city of Philadelphia.

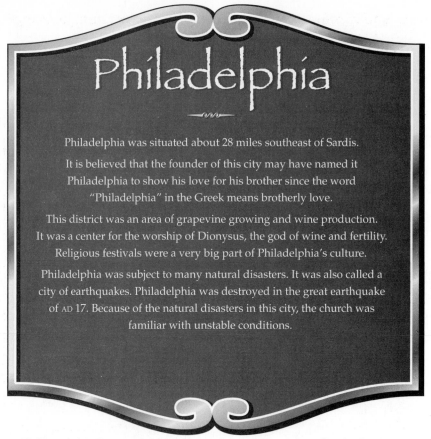

Philadelphia

Philadelphia was situated about 28 miles southeast of Sardis.

It is believed that the founder of this city may have named it
Philadelphia to show his love for his brother since the word
"Philadelphia" in the Greek means brotherly love.

This district was an area of grapevine growing and wine production.
It was a center for the worship of Dionysus, the god of wine and fertility.
Religious festivals were a very big part of Philadelphia's culture.

Philadelphia was subject to many natural disasters. It was also called a
city of earthquakes. Philadelphia was destroyed in the great earthquake
of AD 17. Because of the natural disasters in this city, the church was
familiar with unstable conditions.

Take a look at the large map. Can you find the city of
Philadelphia? Good work! Now look back on page 148 at
Revelation 3:7-13 and fill in the chart on the next page to show
what Jesus says to the church in Philadelphia.

As you continue to fill out your chart, is anything missing?

WHAT section on your chart is blank? *Reproof to the church*

JESUS' MESSAGES TO THE CHURCHES

Church at Philadelphia

Description of Jesus

Revelation 3:7 He who is _____, who is _____, who has the _____ of _____, who _____ and no one will _____, and who _____ and no one _____.

Commendation to the Church (Praise)

Revelation 3:8 I know your _____. Behold, I have _____ before you an _____ _____ which no one can _____, because you have a little _____, and have _____ My _____, and have not _____ My name.

Revelation 3:9 I will make them come and _____ down at your feet, and make them know that I have _____ you.

Reproof Given to the Church

Warnings and Instructions to the Church

Revelation 3:10 I also will _____ you from the _____ of _____, that _____ which is about to come upon the whole _____, to _____ those who dwell on the _____.

Revelation 3:11 I am _____ quickly; _____ _____ what you have so that no one will take your _____.

Promise to the Overcomers

Revelation 3:12 He who overcomes, I will make him a
_____ in the _____ of My God, and he
will not _____ _____ from it anymore; and I will
_____ on him the _____ of My God, and
the _____ of the _____ of My God, the new
_____, which comes down out of _____
from My God, and My new _____.

Wow! Isn't that awesome? Another church that Jesus doesn't correct. Philadelphia is a faithful church. Jesus says the people there have kept His Word and not denied His name. He will make those of the synagogue of Satan bow down to them and know that He loves believers.

Wouldn't you want to be part of this Philadelphia church? They have an open door no one can shut. And they have power. WHAT is an open door—do you know? An open door is the opportunities that God gives us to serve Him and do things for Him, to tell others what we believe about Jesus.

WHAT are the opportunities that God has given you? HOW do you serve Him?

I serve God by being nice to a un saved girl

The name Christian means "little Christ." Is there any way you deny Christ's name in the way you live or the things that you do? _no_ If you answered yes, tell what you do and how you can change.

Now, WHERE did the Philadelphians get that little power? Look up and read Acts 1:8.

Acts 1:8 HOW do we receive power?

_____

Acts 1:8 WHAT are we to do with this power?

_____

Look up and read Ephesians 3:16. HOW is God going to strengthen us? With _____ through _____ _____ in the _____ _____.

God gives us the power we need to be faithful, to persevere, and to do the work that He has for us to do. Look up and read 2 Corinthians 12:9.

WHAT is sufficient for us?

_____

HOW is God's power perfected?

_____

So even when we are weak we have WHAT dwelling in us?

_____

- Are you using the power God has given you? Or do you give up, thinking it is just too hard and you can't do it? _____

  Remember, you can't do it—but God can!

- Is there an open door God wants you to walk through? Will you obey? _____

- Is there someone at school that you know who doesn't have a relationship with Jesus Christ? What's that person's name? _____. You need to tell him or her about Jesus. Could you invite your friend to church or to a Bible study? _____

As we close today, think about the faithfulness of the people at the Philadelphia church. God opens doors that no one can shut. You need to keep His Word by doing all He asks you to do. Even though testing may come, God has the power to see you through it. Hold fast and keep your eyes on Him!

If you overcome, Jesus will make you a pillar in the temple of God, and He will write the name of God, the name of the new Jerusalem, and His new name. You will have access to the city of God, the new Jerusalem. Your new name will identify you with Christ and will allow you entrance to the city of God. You will see God's face!

Why don't you take an empty paper towel tube and paint it to look like a pillar to remind you that if you hold fast and overcome you will enter the new Jerusalem.

Now don't forget to practice your memory verse. Way to go!

ARE YOU HOT, COLD, OR LUKEWARM?

"Hey, guys!" Uncle Jake called out as he headed toward Max, Molly, and Miss Kim. "What's up?"

"Uncle Jake!" cried Max. "You made it back!"

"Sure did. I couldn't wait to get here and see how you like the museum so far. I know Miss Kim is getting you to do your research before you see the exhibits so that what you see won't spoil your joy of discovery."

"We love it!" Molly told Uncle Jake. "We've been working really hard on the seven churches. I never knew how important these letters are and how they pertained to us until we started taking them apart to see what Jesus said to each church."

"That's why I'm so proud of you and Max for being willing to go slow and really study God's Word. God loves us and wants us to be just like Jesus! Miss Kim told me you're going to be making a model of one of the churches. Have you started yet?"

"Not yet," replied Max. "We have one more church to investigate before we can choose our church."

"Then I came at just the right time," Uncle Jake answered. "Making a model of one of the churches sounds like fun."

"But first," Molly said and smiled, "we have to get to work. Let's pray so we can understand Revelation 3 and Jesus' message to the seventh church. Miss Kim said this is a very important message for the church today."

Let's get started, Bible detectives. Pull out your key word bookmark and turn to page 149. Read Revelation 3:14-22 and mark the key words listed on your Observation Worksheet just like they are on your index card. Turn to page 139 if you have lost your card.

Don't forget to mark the pronouns!

To the angel of the church in Laodicea write

Jesus (or any description that refers to Jesus, like *The Amen*)

I know   deeds   love   repent

white garments

He who has an ear, let him hear what the spirit says to the churches

To him who overcomes (or He who overcomes)

Don't forget to mark anything that tells you WHERE by double underlining the WHERE in green.

Turn to page 149. Read Revelation 3:14.

WHAT church is this message for?

_____ Laodicea _____

Look at the museum's plaque to see WHAT it tells us about the city of Laodicea. Watch very closely as you read about this city. Look for how it goes with what Jesus tells them.

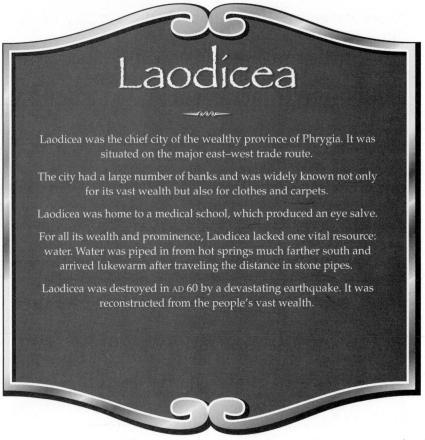

Laodicea

Laodicea was the chief city of the wealthy province of Phrygia. It was situated on the major east–west trade route.

The city had a large number of banks and was widely known not only for its vast wealth but also for clothes and carpets.

Laodicea was home to a medical school, which produced an eye salve.

For all its wealth and prominence, Laodicea lacked one vital resource: water. Water was piped in from hot springs much farther south and arrived lukewarm after traveling the distance in stone pipes.

Laodicea was destroyed in AD 60 by a devastating earthquake. It was reconstructed from the people's vast wealth.

Take a look at the large map on the wall. Can you find the city of Laodicea? All right! Now look back on page 149 at Revelation 3:14-22 and fill in the chart on the next page to show what Jesus says to the church in Laodicea.

As you continue to fill out your chart is anything missing? WHAT section on your chart is blank?

_____

jESUS' MESSAGES TO THE CHURCHES

Church at Laodicea

Description of Jesus

Revelation 3:14 The _____, the _____ and _____ _____, the _____ of the _____ of God.

Commendation to the Church (Praise)

Reproof Given to the Church (What they did wrong)

Revelation 3:15 I know your _____, that you are neither _____ nor _____; I _____ that you were _____ or _____.

Revelation 3:16 Because you are _____, and neither _____ nor _____, I will _____ you out of My _____.

Revelation 3:17 You do not know that you are _____ and _____ and _____ and _____ and _____.

Warnings and Instructions to the Church

Revelation 3:18 I advise you to _____ from Me _____ refined by _____ so that you may become _____, and _____ _____ so that you may _____ yourself, and that the _____ of your nakedness will not be _____; and _____ _____ to _____ your eyes so that you may _____.

Revelation 3:19 Those whom I _____, I _____ and _____; therefore be _____ and _____.

Revelation 3:20 Behold, I stand at the _____ and _____; if anyone _____ My voice and _____ the _____, I will _____ in to him and will _____ with him, and he with Me.

Promise to the Overcomers

Revelation 3:21 He who overcomes, I will grant to him to _____ down with Me on My _____, as I also _____ and sat down with My _____ on His _____.

Isn't it sad? Jesus doesn't have any praise for the church at Laodicea.

Revelation 3:15 WHAT did Jesus tell them their problem was? _____

Revelation 3:16 They are _____

What Jesus is essentially saying to them is "I would rather you be hot—on fire—for Me, to be surrendered, totally committed, to love, obey, and be wholehearted in your devotion. Or be cold, to oppose Me. But do not be lukewarm—neutral, halfhearted, and complacent about being a Christian."

WHAT would it look like to be "hot" for Jesus?

_____

Think about your friends. Are they hot, lukewarm, or cold?

_____

And WHAT about you? WHERE do you fit? _____

_____

When we are lukewarm we are blind to our true condition. The church at Laodicea is deceived into thinking they are something they aren't. They have religion but no relationship with Jesus Christ.

Revelation 3:16 WHAT is Jesus going to do with them?

_____

That word "spit" in the Greek is *emeo,* pronounced em-eh´-o, and it means to vomit. Jesus wants to vomit this church out of His mouth. That doesn't sound very good, does it? Remember what you learned about the water when it reached Laodicea? It was lukewarm. Lukewarm water makes you want to vomit when you drink it.

Did you notice how this very wealthy city thought they were rich but Jesus tells them they are poor?

WHY do you think He tells them they are poor?

_____

Look up and read Colossians 2:2.

WHERE does our wealth come from?

_____

Look up and read 1 Timothy 6:17.

WHAT does Paul tell Timothy to instruct those who are rich not to do?_____

WHAT does he tell them to fix their hope on?

_____

WHAT does the apostle Paul tell us God will do?

_____

Because Laodicea was wealthy, the people thought they had it all together. But they had put their hope in material things rather than the God of all hope. They were blind. Was there any hope for this church?

Yes! That's why Jesus sends this letter—to give them a chance to change. Jesus tells them, "Those whom I love, I reprove and discipline."

Revelation 3:18-19 WHAT does Jesus tell them to do?

_____

_____

Revelation 3:20 WHERE is Jesus?

_____

Isn't that awesome? Jesus is waiting for the people to open the door and let Him come in. Amazing! The Ruler of the universe loves them so much He wants them to sit down on His throne with Him!

- HOW about you? Do you have a relationship with Jesus? Have you opened the door and invited Him into your life? Describe it.

  _____

  _____

- Are you willing to be hot? Are you willing to surrender your life totally to Him? Will you make a decision to put Him first in everything?

  _____

Remember: If you are lukewarm, He will vomit you out of His mouth!

If you haven't invited Jesus into your life and you want to, the first thing you need to do is believe that Jesus is our Savior, that He is God's Son, that He is God, and that He lived a perfect life without sin, and that He died on a cross to pay for our sins. Then He was buried, and God raised Him from the dead.

You also have to know you are a sinner and be willing to confess your sins to God and turn away from them. You have to be willing to turn your entire life over to God to follow Jesus.

You can pray a prayer like this:

Thank You, God, for loving me and sending Your Son Jesus Christ to die for my sins. I am sorry for the things I have done wrong. I am repenting—changing my mind about my sins. Sin is wrong. I don't want to do things my way any more. I want to receive Jesus Christ as my Savior. Now I turn my entire life over to You. Amen.

If you prayed this prayer then you are part of God's family! You are God's child, and Jesus and the Holy Spirit will come to live in you (John 14:23). You now have God's power!

So why don't you go back to the prayer just mentioned and write out today's date—the month, day, and year—next to the "amen" to remind you of the day God saved you from your sins.

Now that you have become part of God's family, you will want to share this great news by telling others (confessing with your mouth) that you believe in Jesus Christ and are now a child of God.

Way to go! We are so very proud of you! You are an overcomer, and Jesus invites you to sit down with Him on His throne. Awesome! You are going to rule with Christ! Draw a picture of you ruling with Jesus on His throne to remind you of this promise!

THE SEVEN CHURCHES

Hey, it's great to have you back at the museum! As we head over to the resource room today, we are going to see how much we remember about the seven churches. Remember that these messages aren't just for the seven churches in Asia; they're also for the church today. God put these messages in His Word so that we can apply them to our lives and live the way He wants us to live.

Don't forget to pray.

Match each church below with the correct description of that church in the column next to it.

1. _e_ Ephesus

2. _c_ Smyrna

3. _f_ Pergamum

4. _b_ Thyatira

5. _g_ Sardis

6. _d_ Philadelphia

7. _a_ Laodicea

a. Lukewarm—vomit out of mouth—no praise

b. Reputation for being alive but actually dead, had religion but no relationship, a few believers didn't soil their garments

c. suffering church—no reproof

d. faithful church—little power —open door for gospel, no reproof

e. endured, didn't allow false teachers but lost their first love

f. held fast to Jesus' name, did not deny their faith but allowed wrong teaching in the church

g. growing church, loving, serving, persevering but tolerated sin in the church (the evil woman)

All right! Now ask yourself: Are the things Jesus praised the churches for seen in my life? Am I willing to suffer for Jesus? Do I need correction? Is there anything in my life I need to change? Do any of Jesus' warnings apply to me? Then go to God and ask Him to forgive you wherever you have fallen short and to help you change the things that need to be changed.

Remember the lessons you have learned from these churches: to stand firm in trials, to remain on fire for Jesus, to love Jesus and others, to teach the truth, to walk through His open door using the opportunities He has given you, to share the gospel, to keep growing in your relationship with Jesus, and to be faithful to Him!

And don't forget to practice your memory verse.

Tomorrow we will find out more about being an overcomer!

Let's have some fun now that we have completed the seven churches. Max, Molly, and Uncle Jake are each going to work on designing their models of the seven churches. You can make a model, too! Just follow the instructions below.

just For Fun

You'll need some construction paper, scissors, glue, markers, colored pencils or crayons, and a small shoebox.

Take the lid off the shoebox and cover it by gluing construction paper on it. Turn the shoebox upside down so that the bottom of the shoebox is facing up. Make a roof for your church with one to two pieces of construction paper, depending on how long your shoebox is. If you need two pieces of paper, glue them together first. Then fold your construction paper in half and fold under about ½" to glue the roof to the flat bottom of the shoebox.

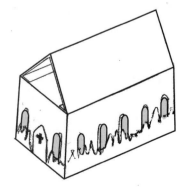

Next, draw or cut out a door on one end of the box. Put windows on both sides of the box.

Now decorate your church by showing the characteristic of the church you've chosen. For example, if you are making the church at Laodicea you could draw a picture of Jesus standing outside the front door and knocking. Use markers, colored pencils, or crayons, and whatever else you want. Be creative and have fun!

WHAT DOES IT TAKE TO BE AN OVERCOMER?

"Hey, Max, I really like your church," Molly said as she looked over Max's model. "It is so cool the way you put the flames around the bottom of the church to show the fire of persecution going on at the church of Smyrna."

"I like yours, too, Molly, especially the way you've drawn Jesus with a heart on His chest, reminding us that He is to be our first love."

"Hey, you two, what about mine?" Uncle Jake smiled. "How do you like the water surrounding the church at Laodicea with Jesus standing at the door and knocking, waiting to be invited in."

"It's awesome, Uncle Jake. This has been so much fun," Max replied. "We'll have to bring mom and dad by so they can see our handiwork."

Miss Kim walked up to admire their churches. "These look great! Let's put them in our display area. Then we have one more very important thing to research before we wrap up Jesus' messages to the churches."

Now that the kids have set up their churches and cleaned up the area, let's pray so we can get to work.

Are you surprised about all you have discovered in Revelation so far? Did you know that each one of these seven churches received all seven letters? Jesus not only had a message for these seven ancient churches, but these messages are also for the church today! Remember Revelation promises us a blessing if we read, hear, and heed the words of the prophecy.

Let's find out what it takes to be an overcomer, to be able to conquer and prevail.

First let's do a cross-reference to find out what we can learn about overcomers.

Look up and read 1 John 5:4-5.

1 John 5:4 WHAT overcomes the world?

_____

WHAT is the victory that has overcome the world?

_____

1 John 5:5 WHO is the one who overcomes the world?

_____

So, from looking at these verses, is every believer (someone who has accepted Jesus Christ as his or her Savior) an overcomer?

_____

Can you be a genuine Christian and not be an overcomer? _____ WHY or WHY not?_____

_____

Look up and read 1 John 3:7-10.

1 John 3:7 WHAT is the one who practices righteousness?

_____

1 John 3:8 WHAT is the one who practices sin?

_____

1 John 3:9 WHAT do you see about the one who is born
of God?

_____

1 John 3:10 HOW is it obvious we are children of God?

_____

Look up and read Titus 1:16.

WHAT do they profess to know?

_____

WHAT do their deeds do?

_____

While we are saved by faith in Jesus Christ (Ephesians 2:8), what we do (our deeds) shows what we really believe. Yes, believers in Jesus still sin, but a child of God cannot continue in (practice) sin, doing the same sin over and over again. If we are genuine believers in Jesus Christ, then there should be a change in us. The things we do should show we believe in Him.

Jesus has overcome this world, and when we accept Him we are born of God and become overcomers. We receive His power to overcome anything big or small—being left out of a group of friends, standing up for what we believe in, being called names, practicing sin such as gossiping, stealing, or cussing.

Jesus gives us the power to overcome hurt, suffering, and hardships, as well as the giving up of our lives if we should be called to stand for Him. Those who truly belong to Jesus are overcomers. They overcome the world because of their faith!

Remember Jesus is coming soon and His reward is with Him (Revelation 22:12)!

Now let's review all the things Jesus promises the overcomers. In the following chart fill in the blanks and draw a picture of what the overcomer receives to help you remember Jesus' promises. You can look back in your book if you need to.

Promises to the Overcomers	
Ephesus Eat of the Tree of life	**Smyrna** Will not be hurt by the Second death
Pergamum Hidden manna, white stone, and a new name	**Thyatira** Authority over the nations I will give him the morning star
Sardis Clothed in white garments, will not erase his name from the book of life.	**Philadelphia** I will make him a pillar in the temple, the name of My God, the name of the new Jerusalem and My new name.
Laodicea Sit down with Jesus on His throne	

Great artwork! Hang on tight because next week you are going to get a glimpse into heaven. That is going to be so cool! Don't forget to say your memory verse to a grown-up this week.

4

THE MYSTERY IN HEAVEN

REVELATION 4–5

It's great to have you back at the museum! Last week you made some amazing discoveries about the seven churches and being an overcomer. Are you ready to uncover the next mystery in Revelation?

This week you are going to get a glimpse into heaven to reveal WHAT is in heaven and WHO is worthy. Doesn't that sound like fun? Let's head back to the resource room so we can find out WHAT John sees next.

WHO IS WORTHY?

"Hey, Molly!" Max called out. "Look at Sam."

"How did he end up with those little pom-pom balls on his nose?" Molly asked as she tried hard not to burst into laughter at Sam's new look.

Max tried to answer as Sam started shaking his head and sneezing. "Someone must have spilled a little glue next to some of the craft supplies. Sam was obviously sniffing for clues inside the cabinet and ended up like this."

Just as Max finished his sentence, Uncle Jake and Miss Kim walked in and stopped in their tracks when they saw Sam running around the room trying to shake off his added whiskers.

"Oh, no," cried Miss Kim. "What happened to Sam?"

Max grinned as he tried to catch Sam. "He's been sniffing out clues that happened to have a little glue on them. Come on, Sam. Come here, boy. Let's get you cleaned up so we can uncover our next mystery."

Now that Sam has calmed down and gotten rid of his pompoms, let's pray so we can get started uncovering the clues for Revelation 4. Let's mark our key words. Pull out your key word bookmark and add the new key words to your index card.

God (draw a purple triangle and color it yellow)

I looked (I saw) (color it blue)

throne (draw and color a blue throne)

worthy (color it purple)

worship (circle in purple and color blue)

Turn to page 151 and read Revelation 4. Mark your new key words and the key words listed below on your Observation Worksheet just like they are on your index card. Turn to page 139 if you have lost your card.

seven Spirits of God (or Spirit) white garments (white robes)

Don't forget to mark the pronouns!

Mark anything that tells you <u>WHERE</u> by double-underlining the <u>WHERE</u> in green. And don't forget to mark anything that tells you WHEN by drawing a green clock or draw a green ○ . Keep your eyes open. There is a very important time phrase in this chapter. Did you find it?

All right! Now let's discover our memory verse this week by looking at the crowns the 24 elders have cast before the throne. On each crown there is a number and a letter. Under the drawing below are blanks for this week's verse with a number under each blank. Find the letter that matches the number in the crowns and write that letter on the blank to solve your memory verse this week.

 __ __ __ __ __ __   __ __ __   __ __ __'   __ __ __
 2 22 10 24 12 14   5 10 19   14 22 15   22 15 10

 __ __ __ __   __ __ __   __ __ __   __ __ __'   __ __
 17 22 10 23   5 20 23   22 15 10   1 22 23   24 22

 __ __ __ __ __ __ __   __ __ __ __ __   __ __ __
 10 19 3 19 9 21 19   1 17 22 10 14   5 20 23

 __ __ __ __ __   __ __ __   __ __ __ __ __ ;
 12 22 20 22 10   5 20 23   4 22 2 19 10

 __ __ __   __ __ __   __ __ __ __ __ __ __   __ __ __
 8 22 10   14 22 15   3 10 19 5 24 19 23   5 17 17

 __ __ __ __ __ __'   __ __ __   __ __ __ __ __ __ __
 24 12 9 20 1 16   5 20 23   18 19 3 5 15 16 19

 __ __   __ __ __ __   __ __ __ __   __ __ __ __
 22 8   14 22 15 10   2 9 17 17   24 12 19 14

 __ __ __ __ __ __ __ ,   __ __ __   __ __ __ __
 19 7 9 16 24 19 23   5 20 23   2 19 10 19

 __ __ __ __ __ __ __ .
 3 10 19 5 24 19 23

Revelation 4:____

Now read Revelation 4 and locate the correct verse number.
Way to go! You did it! Now practice saying this verse to the One who sits on the throne.

FALL DOWN AND WORSHIP

You did great yesterday as you uncovered clues by marking the key words in Revelation 4. Did you notice that your new memory verse solved the mystery of WHO is worthy?

Today let's continue to work on our mystery. Don't forget to pray! Turn to page 151. Let's get the facts of Revelation 4 by asking the 5 W's and an H.

Revelation 4:1 WHEN is this happening? (Did you find this very important time phrase? Did you put a clock over it?)

_____

Revelation 4:1 WHAT does John see?

_____

WHAT does the voice say?

_____

Revelation 4:2 WHERE is John? WHERE is this taking place?

_____

Revelation 4:3 WHAT was the One sitting on the throne like?

_____

Revelation 4:3-4 WHAT was around the throne?

_____

Revelation 4:5 WHAT came out from the throne?

_____

WHAT was before the throne?

_____

WHAT are these seven lamps of fire?

_____

Revelation 4:6 WHAT else was before the throne?

_____

Revelation 4:6-8 Describe the four living creatures.

First creature like a _____

Second creature like a _____

Third creature had a _____ like a _____

Fourth creature like a _____ _____

Each creature had _____ _____ and are full
of _____ around and within.

Revelation 4:8 WHAT do the four living creatures say?

_____

_____

Revelation 4:10 WHAT did the 24 elders do?

_____

Draw what you have just seen in Revelation 4:2-11 in the box
on the next page. Make sure you show what heaven is like, as
well as the people, creatures, and the main event.

Revelation 4:11 WHAT did the 24 elders say? Write this out
for practice since this is your memory verse.

_____

_____

_____

_____

_____

Did you notice that worship is the priority in heaven? WHAT does it mean to worship God? Do you know? Worship means to bow before God. It is to lay flat before God because you recognize He is God and He is to be respected. To respect someone is to hold him or her in high regard, to honor that person. To worship God is to acknowledge God's worth, to honor God as God.

Now think about what is happening on earth today. In general, is worshiping God a priority for those who live on the earth?_____

WHAT is people's general attitude toward God? Is their attitude one of indifference, not really caring about God, or does their attitude show honor? Do they acknowledge WHO God is and bow before Him to give Him glory?

_____

WHAT is your attitude toward God? Do you put Him first? Do you talk about Him to show how important He is to you? HOW do you feel when other people talk badly about Him? _____

_____

Look at Revelation 4:11. WHAT makes God worthy of worship?

_____

God is the One who created all things. The reason we exist is for His will, *not* for our pleasure. The scene in heaven shows us what our lives are to be about. We are to live to do the things that please God, not the things that please us. The way we live should bring honor, glory, and blessing to Him.

Are you doing things to bless and honor God, or do you do the things that break His heart? _____

_____

Name one thing you can change in your life that will help you live for God and His honor rather than yours.

_____

_____

All right! You have just gotten a small glimpse into heaven. What an amazing place! Now before you head out, practice your memory verse to remind yourself of the One who is worthy!

UNCOVERING CLUES: A SEALED BOOK

"Hey, guys, how did you like your glimpse into heaven yesterday?" Miss Kim asked Max and Molly.

"It was so cool," Molly replied.

"Well, are you ready to enter into the museum's room that shows this scene in heaven?"

"We sure are!" Max and Molly both exclaimed. Sam barked his agreement.

"All right then. Let's head down the hallway, past the models of the seven churches. Look for a room on the right that has the word 'Heaven' painted over the doorway. Max, when you're ready, you can open the door that leads to our scene of heaven."

"Wow!" Max and Molly said again as they went through the door and looked in awe at the scene before them. "This is amazing! Look at the throne and the transparent glow on it!" Max cried out.

"Press the first button on the wall, Molly," Miss Kim instructed.

As Molly pushed the button, a beautiful rainbow glittered like a brilliant emerald and surrounded the throne.

"That's fantastic!" Molly laughed.

"Now," Miss Kim replied, "did you notice how many thrones are around God's throne?"

"Twenty-four," Max called out. "And look, there's a gold crown on each throne for the elders to cast before God's throne."

"Right," answered Miss Kim. "When you finish your study

this week, I have a special presentation for you guys right here in heaven. Then once the museum actually opens, there will be special times each day that kids can come into this room and watch the scene from heaven unfold before their eyes. The rest of the time, when there isn't a presentation, they can come in and do things like make the rainbow appear on their own. What do you think about that?"

"That is so wonderful," Max replied. "But what do the rest of these buttons on the panel do?"

"Go ahead and push the next one, Max," Miss Kim said, "and find out." As Max pushed the next button, he and Molly almost jumped out of their skin, while Sam ran around the room barking as peals of thunder boomed overhead and bright flashes of lightning from strobe lights flashed around the throne!

"Whoa!" Max gasped. "I wasn't expecting that. It nearly scared me to death."

"I'll do the next one," Molly said, as she gently pushed the button. Immediately a fiery orange and golden glow came out of each of the seven lamps before the throne. "Cool!" Molly said while clapping her hands. "It's the seven Spirits of God."

Max pushed the next button, and a curtain behind the throne moved to one side to reveal replicas of the four living creatures. Four voices reciting the words of Revelation 4:8 came from the speakers around the room. After they were finished, 24 voices spoke the words of Revelation 4:11.

"I can't believe this!" Max told Miss Kim. "It's like we're really there!"

"I know," Miss Kim smiled. "If you think this is awesome, just think what the real heaven is like. Now we'd better leave heaven and head back to our resource room so you can find out what is happening in Revelation 5. We'll come back after we finish our research and watch our special heaven presentation."

"We can't wait!" Max stated. "Now let's pray so we can find out what happens next!"

Now that we've prayed, pull out your key word bookmark (the index card that you made) and add the new key words listed:

angel (draw blue wings or a blue angel and color it yellow)

book (draw a brown scroll)

seals (color it orange)

Now turn to page 153. Read Revelation 5:1-5, and mark your key words (the new ones just listed and the ones below) on your Observation Worksheets, just like they are on your index card. If you have lost your index card, you can look on page 139 to see how you can mark these words:

God   I looked (or I saw)   throne   worthy   overcome

Jesus (or any description that refers to Jesus, like *the Lion, the Lamb*)

Don't forget to mark the pronouns!

Great work! Now let's find out what is happening in heaven. Read Revelation 5:1-5 on page 153 and answer the 5 W's and an H questions.

Revelation 5:1 WHAT did John see in the hand of Him who sat on the throne?

HOW is it described?

_____

_____

Did you know in Bible times there were no books like we have today? Instead their books were rolled-up paper called scrolls, made of either papyrus or vellum. Did you know that seals were used to close up a scroll? Whenever someone wanted to send a message, he would take hot wax and drop it on the rolled-up scroll. Then he would take his signet ring and press it into the hot wax to form a mark and flatten the wax to keep the scroll closed. People did this to make sure the message would only be opened and read by the person to whom it was being sent.

Revelation 5:2 WHAT did the angel proclaim?

_____

Revelation 5:3-4 WHY was John weeping?

_____

Revelation 5:5 WHO did the elders say was worthy to open the book and its seven seals?

_____

WHY was He worthy?

_____

You have discovered something very important today. You know that God has a sealed book that is written on the inside and on the back, and that Jesus, who is the Lion from the tribe of Judah, has overcome and can open the book. Tomorrow we will find out more about what John saw and the opening of this very important book.

Now practice saying your memory verse to remind yourself of just how awesome God is!

WHO CAN OPEN THE BOOK?

Wow! Wasn't the museum's room in heaven awesome? We can't wait to finish our research this week so we can see the museum's presentation. But before we go back into the heaven room, we need to find out more about God, Jesus, and the sealed-up book.

Let's uncover some more clues. Pray and then turn to page 153. Pull out your key word bookmark and add the new key word listed below to your index card:

prayers (draw a purple ⌣ and color it pink)

Now read Revelation 5:6-10 and mark your new key word and the following key words on your Observation Worksheets, just like they are on your index card. Turn to page 139 if you have lost your card.

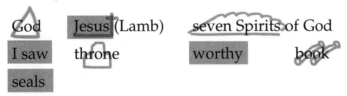

God   Jesus (Lamb)   seven Spirits of God

I saw   throne   worthy   book

seals

Don't forget to mark the pronouns!

You did great! Now read Revelation 5:6-10 and ask the 5 W's and an H.

Revelation 5:6 WHAT did John see between the throne with the four living creatures and the elders?

_____

WHAT are the seven horns and seven eyes on the Lamb?

_____

Revelation 5:7 WHAT did the Lamb do?

_____

Revelation 5:8 WHAT did the four living creatures and the 24 elders do?

_____

_____

WHAT is in the golden bowls?

_____

Do you think that prayer is important since it is in these bowls in heaven? _____

Draw a picture of what John sees in Revelation 5:6-8 in the box below.

Revelation 5:9 WHY was the Lamb worthy to break its seals?

_____

_____

Revelation 5:10 WHAT are those who have been

purchased by Jesus' blood (those who are Christians) made to be?

_____

WHAT will they do?

_____

Isn't this awesome? God has made us a kingdom and priests to rule and reign on the earth. Stop and think about it. You are going to be a ruler. You are going to rule on the earth! Isn't that amazing?

Do you remember WHAT God told Adam and Eve to do back in Genesis 1:28 after He created them? Look up and read Genesis 1:27-28.

WHAT did God tell Adam and Eve to do?

Be _____ and _____, and _____ the earth, and _____it; and _____ over the fish of the sea and over the birds of the sky and over _____ _____ _____ that moves on the _____.

Adam and Eve were to rule over the earth. God created the earth to belong to mankind, but something happened to change that. Do you remember WHAT happened? Look up and read Genesis 3:3-6.

Genesis 3:6 WHAT did Adam and Eve do?

_____

Read Genesis 3:24 WHAT happened to man?

_____

When Adam and Eve disobeyed God and ate the fruit in Genesis 3, sin entered the world. To sin is to disobey God. It is to know the right thing to do and not do it (James 4:17). To sin is to not believe what God says.

Once Adam sinned, sin was passed from one generation to the next generation. It was like sin was in our genes, in our DNA. The Bible says in Romans 5:12, "Therefore, just as through one man sin entered into the world, and death through sin, and so death spread to all men, because all sinned." When Adam sinned, he passed his sin on to everyone born after him. Because of sin, mankind lost his right to rule over the earth.

Can you believe that Jesus would leave heaven to save us from our sins? Jesus came to earth as a human being, but He was born without Adam's "sin" genes because He was born of a virgin mother and His father was God! Jesus became a human being so He could redeem us (buy us back) from Satan with His precious blood! Man lost his right to rule the earth to Satan in the garden of Eden, but Jesus, as a man without sin, died on a cross to pay for our sins. Then He rose from the dead—defeating sin, death, and Satan—to give us back our right to rule and reign with Him on earth.

WHAT kind of animal is used to describe Jesus in Revelation 5:6-12? Do you wonder why Jesus is called a lamb? It's because the blood of a lamb was used during one of the plagues God sent when Pharaoh would not let God's people leave Egypt.

God told the children of Israel to kill a lamb, take its blood, and put it on the doorposts of their houses. Then when the angel of death came to kill all of the firstborn in Egypt, he would pass over the houses that had the blood of the lamb on the doorposts (Exodus 12:1-13). This "Passover" is a picture of what Jesus would do for us when He died for our sins!

Did you know that Jesus was crucified on the very day of Passover, when all the Passover lambs were being killed for the Passover feast? Jesus is the perfect Lamb without blemish who was slain so we could have eternal life. That's why we see Jesus as the slain Lamb in Revelation 5. Because Jesus paid for our sins with His blood, He is the only One worthy to open the book and break its seals.

One day very soon, the Lamb of God will take the book and break its seals so we can get back the right to rule that Adam and Eve lost when they disobeyed God and believed Satan. Isn't it exciting to know that one day, if you belong to Jesus, you will rule and reign on earth? Unbelievable!

As you head out today, don't forget to practice saying your memory verse.

WORSHIP THE LAMB

"Good morning, Miss Kim!" Max called out as he and Molly entered the resource room.

"Good morning, guys. Are you ready to wrap up Revelation 5 today?"

"We sure are!" Molly replied. "All we can talk about is how once we're finished we will get to see the presentation in the heaven room."

"I hope you like it! Why don't we pray so you can get to work? Yesterday you uncovered some pretty amazing things about the Lamb being worthy to open the book. Today you will discover more about the Lamb and worship," Miss Kim said.

"That sounds awesome!" Max answered. "I'll pray."

Okay, Bible detectives, get to work. Find out what is happening in heaven. Read Revelation 5:11-14 on page 154 and mark the following key words that are on your bookmark:

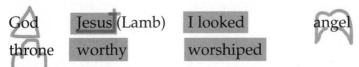

God   Jesus (Lamb)   I looked   angel

throne   worthy   worshiped

Don't forget the pronouns, and don't forget to mark anything that tells you WHEN with a green clock 🕐 or a green ◯.

Now turn back to Revelation 5:11-14 on page 154 and answer the 5 W's and an H.

Revelation 5:11-12 WHAT did John hear?

_____

_____

Revelation 5:14 WHAT is another word for praising God? What are the elders doing in verse 14?

_____

Isn't this awesome? Once again we see worship in heaven to God and the Lamb.

Revelation 5:13 WHAT will God and the Lamb have forever?

_____

Dominion means "power and strength." This shows us that God and Jesus' power and strength will be forever. God will take His great power and begin to reign visibly with His Son! Don't forget: If you are a child of God—a believer in relationship with Jesus—then you are going to get to rule with Him! Isn't that amazing?

Have you noticed that everyone who sees God and the Lamb as they really are can't help but call out, "Worthy, worthy, worthy" in worship? Can you imagine what it will be like when we finally see God face-to-face?

Why don't you write a prayer of praise on the lines below to worship God and Jesus, to thank them for WHO they are and WHAT they have done for you?

_____

_____

_____

_____

_____

Are you ready to live in a way that brings honor and blessing to God and His Son? Remember, one day you will rule and reign with Jesus. Live as an overcomer until He comes!

Way to go! We are so proud of you for doing this study! Keep up the good work. Don't forget to practice saying your memory verse today. Say it to God and Jesus, who are worthy to be worshiped and praised!

5

THE BREAKING OF THE SEALS

REVELATION 6–7

It's great to have you back at the museum! How did you like your glimpse into heaven? Wasn't it amazing! So far we have unveiled some awesome discoveries. In Revelation 1 we discovered that God gave the Book of Revelation to His bond-servants through John so that we would know what was going to happen in the future.

In Revelation 2–3 we uncovered Jesus' messages to the churches and how to apply those messages to our lives.

Then in Revelation 4–5 we got a glimpse into heaven and the worship before the throne. We saw Jesus as He prepares to take the book (the scroll) from God's hand and break its seven seals.

WHAT is so important about this sealed-up book? Wait until you find out! If you didn't know God, the future would be flat-out scary. As these seals are broken, you will discover events that frighten a lot of people because the seals bring about a lot of pain and destruction. You need to remember that if you belong to Jesus, you have nothing to fear. You can relax because Jesus has already rescued you. Your future is secure in Him.

Are you ready to watch the Lamb? Then let's head back to watch the scene in heaven unfold!

COME!

"Wow!" Max exclaimed as he, Molly, Uncle Jake, and Miss Kim walked out of the heaven room. "That was soooo awesome! I got chill bumps, and my skin tingled as the 24 elders got up from the throne, laid down their crowns, and fell down in worship. That was some presentation."

"Especially the four living creatures," Molly joined in. "Those were some pretty amazing costumes. I was a little scared as they came out from behind the curtain to worship God. I thought the room was fantastic when we visited it the first time with all the special effects, but having real people come in and play the parts was unbelievable!"

"I'm glad it had that effect on you." Miss Kim smiled. "That's what we hope everyone will experience as they watch our special show. There is no way we can actually show what it would really be like in heaven, but we hope to at least give people an idea what it might be."

"My favorite part," Max told Miss Kim, "was when John was weeping and, as the elder tells him to stop because the Lion of Judah has overcome, we see Jesus as the slain Lamb walk in and take the book out of God's hand. That was so cool!"

Molly asked Miss Kim, "Will we get to see what happens when the Lamb breaks the seals?"

"We are working on a special video presentation to play on a big screen in the next room, but you can't go in until you discover for yourself what happens when the Lamb breaks the seals."

"All right!" squealed Molly. "Let's get back to work on our research. Race you to the resource room, Max."

"You're on," Max replied as he took off running.

Let's pray before we see what happens in Revelation 6. Okay, now turn to page 155. Read Revelation 6:1-8 and mark the following key words from your bookmark on your Observation Worksheet:

God   Jesus (Lamb)   I looked (I saw)   seals

Don't forget to mark the pronouns! And remember to mark anything that tells you WHEN with a green clock or a green ◯.

Great work! Before we wrap up our research for today, you need to uncover this week's memory verse by looking at the rebus. A rebus is a word puzzle that mixes pictures and words. When you combine the pictures and the letters by adding or subtracting letters, you will end up with a new word.

Write the solution on the lines underneath the puzzle. Then look at Revelation 7 on page 157 to discover the verse reference.

_____

_____

_____

_____

_____

Revelation 7:___

Don't forget to practice saying this verse three times today!

THE MYSTERY OF THE FIRST FOUR SEALS

You did a wonderful job yesterday as you marked key words to reveal what happens in heaven as the Lamb (Jesus) takes the book. Today you are going to solve the mystery of the first four seals as you ask the 5 W's and an H questions. Don't forget to pray, and then turn to page 155. Read Revelation 6:1-8 to reveal WHAT happens when the Lamb breaks the seals.

Revelation 6:1 WHAT did John see?

The _____ broke one of the _____ _____.

WHEN the first seal was broken, WHAT did one of the four living creatures say? What did its voice sound like?

_____! With a voice of _____

Revelation 6:2 WHAT did John see when the first seal was broken?

A _____ _____

WHAT do we see about the rider of this horse?

He had a _____; and a _____ was given to him.

WHAT did he go out to do?

To _____

Did you notice anything unusual about the rider of this horse?

He has a bow, but does he have any arrows to shoot?

_____

We see he is wearing a crown, and that he goes out to conquer—but he is conquering without a weapon. This could mean that he conquers using peace and diplomacy rather than by using military strength.

WHO do you think this rider of the white horse might be? Do you know of anyone in the end times WHO will bring about peace first in order to conquer? Have you ever studied the Book of Daniel?

_____

WHO do you think this rider could be?

_____

Revelation 6:3-4 WHAT did John see when the second seal was broken?

A _____ horse went out.

WHAT was granted to its rider?

To _____ _____ from the _____

WHAT was given to this rider?

A _____ _____

If this rider is granted the power to take peace from the earth, does that mean there has to be peace in order for it to be taken away? Yes, you can't take away something you don't have. Since the second rider takes away peace, does it make sense that the first rider on the white horse was the one to *bring* peace?

When we don't have peace, what do we usually have? WHAT is the opposite of peace and is fought with weapons? ___ ___ ___

Is this what the second rider could be bringing?_____

Revelation 6:5 WHAT did John see when the Lamb broke the third seal?

A _____ horse

WHAT did the rider have in his hand?

A pair of _____

Revelation 6:6 WHAT did the voice say?

"A quart of _____ for a _____, and three quarts of _____ for a denarius; and do not damage the _____ and the _____."

WHAT do we see in this rider's hand? A pair of scales, which would be used to weigh and measure food. Did you know that a denarius is a day's wage? That means you'd have to work all day to buy a quart of wheat! Food must be scarce to be so expensive. WHAT do you think this rider might bring that has to do with a shortage of food? F __ m __ __ e

Do you know that after war there is often lack of food?

Revelation 6:7-8 WHAT did John see when the fourth seal was broken?

An _____ horse

WHAT name did the rider have?

_____

WHAT was following after the rider?

_____

WHAT was given to them?

"_____ was given to them over a _____ of the _____, to _____ with _____ and with _____ and with _____ and by the wild _____ of the earth."

WHAT does the fourth rider bring?_____

We see that this rider is given the authority to kill a fourth of the people on earth. WHERE will these that are killed go? Do you know? WHAT is following death?

_____

This seems to show that the fourth of the people of the earth who are killed are not saved and will go to Hades, where the lake of fire is. How awful!

Did you notice something very important in this verse? How about the fact that this rider is *given* authority to kill? This means the rider is not the one in control. God allows the rider to kill. God is in control.

Now go back and find all the words from each of the blanks (starting at the beginning of "Day Two" in this week) and circle them in the word search below.

T	E	A	D	C	R	H	T	A	E	D	Y	B	O	W
S	C	U	E	O	E	S	T	S	A	E	B	P	S	i
i	N	T	N	N	D	N	S	E	L	A	C	S	X	N
R	E	H	A	q	N	G	i	R	F	A	M	i	N	E
H	L	O	R	U	U	H	A	M	H	T	k	E	S	H
C	i	R	i	E	H	B	T	T	A	W	C	A	E	S
i	T	i	U	R	T	C	A	R	L	F	A	R	A	A
T	S	T	S	Y	F	E	R	P	U	M	L	T	L	S
N	E	Y	S	E	D	A	H	O	E	O	B	H	S	E
A	P	E	A	R	T	H	D	E	W	A	F	T	E	V
H	A	D	E	S	R	O	H	R	G	N	C	A	T	E
E	S	N	E	S	W	O	R	D	O	K	N	E	i	N
L	A	M	B	E	k	A	T	L	i	W	T	H	H	D
q	O	R	E	D	R	A	W	L	i	T	S	W	W	G
C	X	X	D	R	i	O	L	G	i	O	P	H	T	W

Great work! Did you notice that while the Lamb is breaking the seals in heaven, the events that unfold are happening on the earth? WHO is in control over all these horrible events? God! The things we have uncovered today are very scary to some people, but we have to remember that God is the One in control. He alone has all authority and power in His hand!

Did you know that the breaking of these seals is the beginning of God's judgment on the earth? Yes, God is a God of salvation. He is loving, forgiving, and merciful. But He is also a holy God who must judge sin. These judgments that are coming are to put an end to sin.

One question you may be asking is "If I am a Christian, will I be on the earth when these judgments come?" You have probably heard about a very important event that Christians call the "rapture." The word *rapture* isn't used in the Bible, but it means to be carried away in body or caught up to heaven.

Christians use the word *rapture* to refer to the event that is talked about in 1 Thessalonians 4:16-17. These verses say that Jesus will one day descend from heaven with a shout and catch those who are alive plus the people already dead in Christ together in the clouds to meet Him in the air.

WHEN will this "rapture" (the catching-up of believers) take place and the people who haven't accepted Jesus as their Savior be left behind on earth? The Bible gives us clues, but it doesn't give an exact time WHEN this event will happen. Different Bible scholars have different opinions. That's why it is so important for us to study the Bible for ourselves!

Don't worry over WHEN the rapture will happen. Just know that if you are a believer in Jesus Christ, your future in heaven is secure. Revelation 3:10 tells us that we will be kept from the hour of testing that is about to come upon the whole world. So set your heart, faithful and valiant warrior, on living for Him!

One day very soon the trumpet will sound, Jesus will descend from heaven with a shout, and you will meet Him in the air to live with Him forever! Don't be afraid of the horrible events to come. God is telling us in His Word what will happen so we can be prepared for the future. That way we can share what we know with other people. Put your trust in Jesus!

Now that you have uncovered some very important truths, how would you like to make one of the awesome horses in Revelation 6? Did you know that people call the riders of these horses the four riders of the apocalypse? There are four horses for the four riders of the apocalypse. Pretty cool, huh? Especially since the Greek word for revelation is *apokalupsis*.

Here's how Max and Molly are each going to make one of the four horses of the apocalypse at the museum. You will need these supplies: wallpaper paste (non-toxic), newspaper, scissors or a craft knife, white primer, acrylic paint, material to make your form (such as a water bottle), metal hangers with cardboard tubing at the bottom, a piece of cardboard, and clear mailing tape.

First make the body from your form. (Look at the diagram on page 119.) Next draw and cut out a horse's head from cardboard.

Attach it to the water bottle with clear tape. Cut holes in the bottom of the bottle and back to stick in the cardboard tubes to make the legs and tail. Be very careful cutting the holes. You may need a grown-up to help you.

Next mix up the wallpaper paste according to the instructions. You need approximately two cups of paste in a large bowl. Let it stand for 15 minutes.

Tear newspaper into strips one inch wide and six inches long. Thoroughly wet the newspaper strips with wallpaper paste. Take the strips and place them on the form. Layer the strips in a random pattern and overlap them. When you have finished, let your horse dry completely for one to two days.

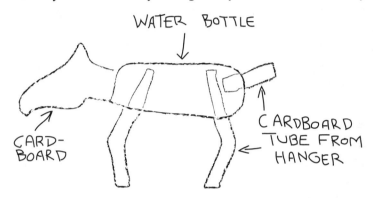

Then you can use a white primer to cover the horse as a base coat. After the primer is dry, paint your horse with acrylic paint. Be creative and have fun!

Before you head out, don't forget to practice your memory verse this week!

THE EARTH IS SHAKEN!

"Hey, Max! How do you like my white horse?" Molly asked as she added the finishing touches.

"It looks great." Max smiled. "I like the way you put the crown on the horse's head. Where are you going to put the bow?"

"I think I'm going to glue it on his side close to his neck. How about you? Where are you going to put the sword that goes with the red horse?"

"I think I'll put it right here on his side," Max answered as he glued the sword in place.

About that time Miss Kim walked into the resource room with Uncle Jake.

"Hey, guys, you have done an awesome job on those horses. How would you like to head down the hallway to see our video presentation?" Miss Kim asked.

"That sounds like fun!" Max responded. "Let's put our horses on display on the way down there. I can't wait to see the four horses in action in the movie."

"Our video guys put in some fantastic special effects to show what these four horses represent as they gallop onto the scene, so it may be a little intense. We also have something fun that kids can do while they watch the video. They can make the special sound effects of the galloping horses as they appear on the screen."

"That sounds like fun. How do we do it?" Molly asked as they walked into the room with a huge video screen.

"Come over here to this table. We have some coconut shells like they used to use in radio and the movies to make the noise of horses galloping. You take the shells and hit the table in rhythm with them like this when you see the horses appear on-screen. Another way to make horse noises is to use plastic or paper cups."

"This is fun," Max said as he practiced his galloping techniques. "How about we each do two horses?"

"No way!" Uncle Jake joined in. "You have to let me do at least one."

"Okay, Uncle Jake, you can go first!" Max said as he handed Uncle Jake the coconut shells. Miss Kim pushed the button to start the video.

Kids, did you make the galloping noises, too? Wasn't that fun?

Okay, let's pray and get started. Now let's take a minute to review.

HOW many seals are there on the book? _____

HOW many has the Lamb opened so far? _____

Do you remember the colors of all four horses?

_____, _____, _____, and

_____.

Let's find out what happens next!

Add the following new key words to your bookmark:

earthquake (draw a brown 〰)

wrath (draw a red \/)

Now turn to page 156. Read Revelation 6:9-17 and mark on your Observation Worksheets your new key words above and the ones listed below from your bookmark:

God   Jesus (Lamb)   I looked (I saw)   seals

white robe   throne   those [all] who dwell on the earth

Don't forget to mark the pronouns and anything that tells you <u>WHERE</u> by double-underlining the <u>WHERE</u> in green. And don't forget to mark anything that tells you WHEN with a green clock: ⏰ or green ◯.

Now let's uncover the next two seals. Ask the 5 W's and an H for Revelation 6:9-17.

Revelation 6:9 WHAT did John see when the fifth seal was opened?

_____

These souls that are under the altar are martyrs. Do you

remember what it means to be a martyr? A martyr is a witness. It is someone who chooses to die rather than give up what he or she believes in. A martyr is someone who is killed for his faith. Remember Polycarp (see Week 2, Day 3)?

WHY were the people underneath the altar slain in Revelation 6:9?

_____

These martyrs gave up their lives for the cause of Jesus Christ!

Revelation 6:10 WHAT did they cry out?

_____

_____

Revelation 6:11 WHAT were they given?

_____

WHAT were they told?

_____

WHY were they told this?

_____

_____

Does that sound like other people will die for their faith in Jesus before everything is finished? It sure does. Do you remember what Jesus says in Matthew 10:39? "He who has found his life will lose it, and he who has lost his life for My sake will find it."

We can deny Christ and live selfishly for a while, but in the end we will die—and by not believing in Christ, we will have lost our lives forever. But when we give our lives for the sake of Jesus, our lives aren't lost because Jesus gives us eternal life.

Jesus will avenge the blood of those who give up their lives for His sake in His perfect timing. But those who give up their lives for Him will live forever with Him.

Revelation 6:12-14 WHAT did John see when the sixth seal was broken?

There was a great _____, the sun became _____, the moon became like _____, the stars of the sky _____ to the _____, the sky was _____ _____ like a scroll, and every mountain and island were _____ out of their places.

Revelation 6:15 WHAT did the kings of the earth and the great men and the commanders and the rich and the strong and every slave and free man do?

_____

Revelation 6:16 WHAT did they say to the mountains and to the rocks? _____

_____

Revelation 6:17 WHAT day had come?

_____

WHOSE wrath was it?

_____

WHEN did this event take place? WHAT seal has been broken?

_____

Pretty scary isn't it? Earthquakes, the sun turning black, the moon turning like blood, stars falling, the sky being split apart, and mountains and islands being moved from their places.

Did you notice that all of the men who hid themselves know WHO is bringing this calamity about? But instead of turning to God, WHAT do they ask for? To be hid from His presence and wrath! God has brought about some pretty cataclysmic events to get their attention, but all they want to do is run away from God instead of changing their ways and running *to* Him.

HOW about you? Has there been a time when God wanted to get your attention, but instead of listening to what He wanted, you turned the other way?

Should you be scared when it looks like the world is falling apart? No. You should remember that God is the One who sits on the throne and turn to Him.

You did an incredible job today looking at some frightening events to come, at people giving up their lives for the sake of Jesus, and then watching God shake the world up with some amazing events!

Before you head out today, turn to page 155 of your Observation Worksheets, and underline in orange the number of each one of the seven seals you have seen so far in Revelation 6. Write the number of each seal in the margin next to the verse that tells about that seal.

All right! Way to go! As we close, don't forget to practice your memory verse. As you say it aloud, let it remind you that you do not need to fear what is coming because the Lamb is the One in the center of the throne. He will be your Shepherd. Jesus will guide you to the water of life and wipe every tear from your eyes.

FOUR ANGELS AT THE
FOUR CORNERS OF THE EARTH

It's great to have you back at the museum! How did you like going into the room with the altar after you finished the video? Were you surprised when Max pushed the button on the wall and heard the souls crying out to the Lord?

And in the next room Sam really barked when the sixth seal was broken and the room shook because of the earthquake. Did you feel it too? Molly liked sliding the black film over the sun and the red film over the moon. And when the glittery stars fell from the sky, Uncle Jake jumped. I bet you did too! The Discovery Bible Museum is such an amazing and fun place!

Let's head back to the resource room to find out what happens after we hear the people on earth proclaim that the great day of their wrath has come. Are you ready? Great! Why don't you pray and then turn to page 157. Pull out your keyword bookmark and add the new key word:

seal, sealed (this is different from the seven seals on the book—draw a purple S)

Now read Revelation 7:1-8 and mark your new key word and the key words listed below on your Observation Worksheets. Don't forget: If you have lost your bookmark, you can turn to page 31 for instructions or page 139.

God angel

Don't forget to mark the pronouns. Anything that tells you <u><u>WHERE</u></u>, double-underline the <u><u>WHERE</u></u> in green, and mark anything that tells you WHEN by drawing a green clock  or a ○ .

Those were some great observations! Now let's find out what these angels are up to by asking the 5 W's and an H for Revelation 7:1-8.

Revelation 7:1 WHAT did John see?_____

_____

Look back at Revelation 6:12. WHEN is this happening? WHAT seal has been broken?

_____

Revelation 7:2 WHAT did John see and WHAT did he have?

_____

HOW many angels does this make? _____

Revelation 7:3 WHAT does this angel tell the other angels?

_____

_____

Revelation 7:4 HOW many people are to be sealed?

_____

WHO are they?

_____

Revelation 7:5-8 Name the 12 tribes of Israel.

_____

_____

_____

HOW many from each tribe were sealed?

_____

Wow! You have discovered one of the two different groups of people that are mentioned in Revelation 7 today. This group is the 144,000 from the tribes of the sons of Israel, bond-servants of God, whom God will seal before the angels harm the earth.

Tomorrow we will find out WHO the other group of people is that John sees. Don't forget to practice your memory verse!

A GREAT MULTITUDE

It's great to have you back at the resource room. Watch out! Sam is pretty excited to see you and eager to lick your face. He is ready to solve the mystery of the second group of people mentioned in Revelation 7. How about you?

Why don't you pray, and then turn to page 159? Pull out your keyword bookmark and add this new key word:

tribulation (box it in black)

Let's solve the mystery of the people mentioned in Revelation 7. Read Revelation 7:9-17 and mark your new key word and the key words listed below on your Observation Worksheet:

God　　Jesus (Lamb)　　I looked　　angel

throne　　worshiped

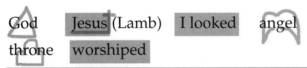

white robe, washed their robes and made them white

Don't forget to mark the pronouns. Also mark anything that tells you WHEN by drawing a green clock or a ○ .

Now answer the 5 W's and an H questions.

Revelation 7:9 WHAT is the other group of people mentioned in this verse?

_____

WHO are they? Are they Jews like the 144,000? WHERE do they come from?

_____

_____

WHERE are they standing?

_____

HOW are they clothed?

_____

WHAT do they have in their hands?

_____

Revelation 7:13-14 WHERE have these people come from?

_____

Are these (the great multitude) believers? _____

HOW do you know?

_____

Revelation 7:15-17 Have these believers in Jesus suffered during this great tribulation? _____ Explain your answer using verses 15-17.

_____

_____

_____

From what you have seen today, even in the great tribulation will there be people who are saved? _____

_____

Revelation 7:17 WHAT will the Lamb do for them? See if you can answer this without looking, since this is your memory verse.

_____

_____

Wow! You have discovered two different groups of people this week. Yesterday you saw that the first group, the 144,000, were from the tribes of the sons of Israel. Today you discovered that the other group is the great multitude made up of all tribes, tongues, and nations who have washed their robes in the Lamb's blood and will suffer in the great tribulation. But because they are saved, they will come out of their suffering and will worship and serve God in His temple. God will spread His tabernacle (sanctuary or shelter) over them, and the Lamb will lead them and wash every tear from their eyes. Isn't that awesome? God has an amazing plan. He is a God of salvation!

See if you can remember each one of the six seals you have studied so far. Draw a picture of each of the seals that you have investigated in the chart on the next page. Make sure you add all the details (for example, if you are drawing one of the horses, show what the rider of the horse is carrying). You can go back and look in your book if you aren't sure of all the details.

The Seven Seals

First Seal	Second Seal
_____ horse Brings _____	_____ horse Brings _____
Third Seal	**Fourth Seal**
_____ horse Brings _____	_____ horse _____ and _____
Fifth Seal	**Sixth Seal**
_____ under the _____	earthquake, _____ , moon, _____ The great day of _____

Seventh Seal

_____ in heaven, angels given _____ _____

Great artwork! Now, HOW many seals are there on this sealed-up book? _____

HOW many seals have been broken—HOW many have you uncovered so far? _____

HOW many are left? _____

That's right. You have one more seal to discover along with a lot more exciting events in Revelation 8–22 as God unfolds His plan for the future. Six seals have been broken bringing about peace, war, famine, death, martyrs, a great earthquake, the sun as black as sackcloth, the moon like blood, stars falling to earth, the sky splitting like a scroll with every mountain and island moved out of their places, and people hiding themselves in caves, rocks, and mountains crying out to be hid from the presence of God and the wrath of the Lamb!

WHAT will happen next? Will things get worse? WHEN will Jesus come with the clouds? WHO will win the war of the Lamb—the battle of good against evil?

Hang on tight! You'll find out as you continue to solve the mystery of Revelation in Max, Molly, and Sam's adventure *A Sneak Peek into the Future,* where they explore Revelation 8–22. The wrath of the Lamb has come. Join Max and Molly as they discover WHAT happens after the sixth seal.

To give you a taste of what is to come and let you finish the chart on page 130, read the first six verses of Revelation 8:

> *When the Lamb broke the seventh seal, there was silence in heaven for about half an hour. And I saw the seven angels who stand before God, and seven trumpets were given to them. Another angel came and stood at the altar, holding a golden censer; and much incense was given to him, so that he might add it to the prayers of all the saints on the golden altar which was before the throne. And the smoke of the incense, with the prayers of the saints, went up before God out of the angel's hand. Then the angel took the censer and filled it with the fire of the altar, and threw it to the earth; and there followed peals of thunder and sounds and flashes of lightning and an earthquake. And the seven angels who had the seven trumpets prepared themselves to sound them.*

Now, fill in the blanks on your chart and draw this last seal.

AWESOME! We can't wait to find out WHAT happens next! We are so proud of you!

THE MYSTERY UNFOLDS

Wow! You did it! You have begun to unravel the mystery of Revelation. Just look at all you have discovered in only seven chapters of Revelation. You know WHO gave the revelation, HOW it was given, and WHY it was given—so God could show us what is going to happen in the future. Absolutely amazing!

You also uncovered Jesus' messages to the seven churches in Asia and learned that these messages are also for you. You have examined your heart to see if you are living the way God wants you to. You saw that you have a choice to accept Jesus as your Savior. Jesus is patiently waiting for you to invite Him in. Isn't it awesome how much God and Jesus love you? God has an amazing plan. He is a God of salvation!

You also discovered that if you are a believer in Jesus Christ, you are an overcomer and have nothing to fear because a loving God holds you in the palm of His hand. He is in control of all your circumstances!

You got a glimpse into heaven and saw the worship before the throne with some pretty amazing creatures. You saw that Jesus is the only One worthy to break the seven seals on the book. Then you heard the gallop of the horses as Jesus breaks the first seal and God's judgments begin on those who dwell on the earth.

As we wrap up this adventure there is so much more to discover before the mystery of Revelation is solved. Don't forget to join Max, Molly, and Sam in the rest of their Revelation adventure—*A Sneak Peek into the Future!* Find out all that happens when the seventh seal is broken and the seven trumpets sound. HOW many more judgments are there? WHO is the beast that comes out of the abyss? WHAT will happen to the two witnesses? And WHEN will Jesus come again?

Just remember that God is in control. He has shown you what will happen in His Word. And He is faithful. You can trust Him!

Don't forget to go to www.precept.org/D4Ycertificate and print out your certificate for standing firm and persevering to the end. We are so very proud of you! Keep up the good work. See you back at The Discovery Bible Museum in the next book, *A Sneak Peek into the Future,* to finish our Revelation adventure in God's Word!

Molly, Max, and

(Sam)

Sarah

PUZZLE ANSWERS

Page 12

> <u>Blessed</u> is <u>he</u> who <u>reads</u> and <u>those</u> who <u>hear</u> the <u>words</u> of the <u>prophecy</u>, and <u>heed</u> the <u>things</u> which are <u>written</u> in <u>it</u>; for the <u>time</u> <u>is</u> <u>near</u>.
>
> Revelation 1:<u>3</u>

Page 37

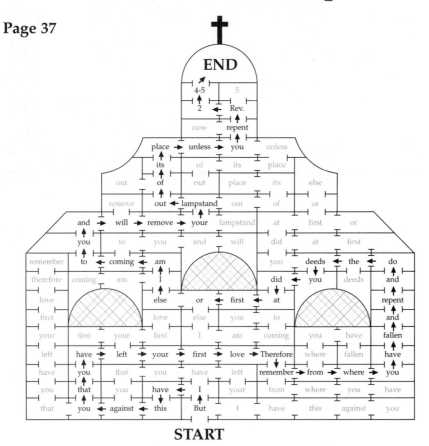

START

"But I have this against you, that you have left your first love. Therefore remember from where you have fallen, and repent and do the deeds you did at first; or else I am coming to you and will remove your lampstand out of its place—unless you repent."

Revelation 2:<u>4</u>-<u>5</u>

Pages 38-39

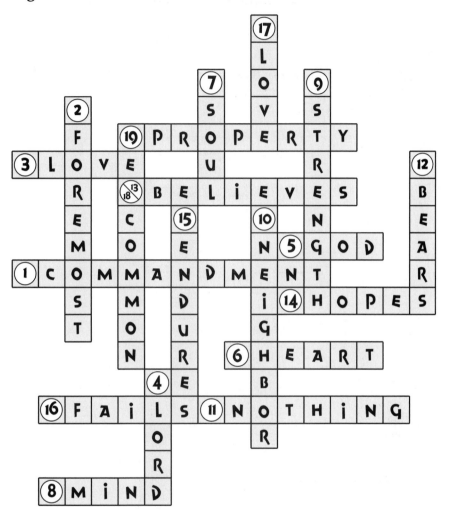

Page 71

"Who is the one who overcomes the world, but he who believes that Jesus is the Son of God?"

1 John 5:<u>5</u>

Page 86

1. <u>e</u>, Ephesus   2. <u>c</u>, Smyrna   3. <u>f</u>, Pergamum
4. <u>g</u>, Thyatira   5. <u>b</u>, Sardis   6. <u>d</u>, Philadelphia
7. <u>a</u>, Laodicea

Page 94

Worthy are You, our Lord and our God, to receive glory and honor and power; for You created all things, and because of Your will they existed, and were created.

Revelation 4:<u>11</u>

Page 112

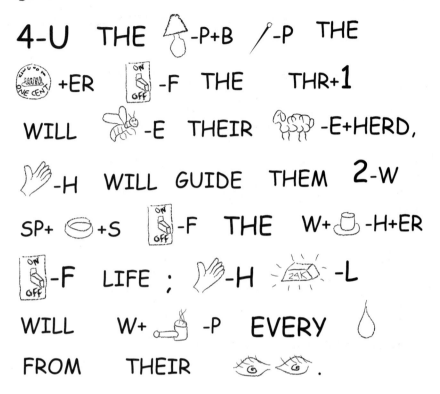

For the Lamb in the center of the throne will be their shepherd, and will guide them to springs of the water of life; and God will wipe every tear from their eyes.

Revelation 7:<u>17</u>

Page 116

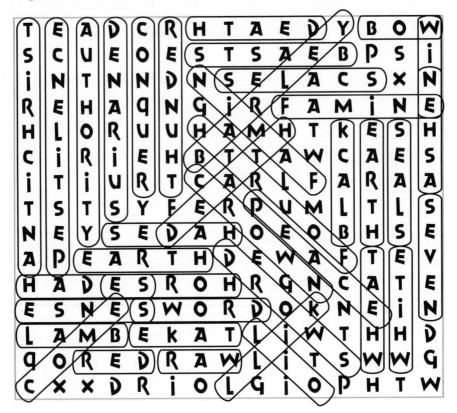

Antichrist	Earth	Scales
Ashen	Earth	Seals
Authority	Famine	Sense
Barley	Famine	Seven
Beasts	Fourth	Sword
Black	Hades	Sword
Bow	Hades	Take
Care	Horse	Thunder
Come	Kill	War
Conquer	Lamb	Wheat
Crown	Oil	White
Death	Peace	Wine
Death	Pestilence	
Denarius	Red	

KEY WORD LIST FOR REVELATION 1-7

To the angel of the church in (Ephesus, etc.) (color orange)

Jesus (or any description that refers to Jesus, like *The One, the Lion, the Lamb,* and any pronouns) (draw a purple cross and color the word yellow)

I know (underline in red and color it yellow)

deeds (draw and color green feet)

love (draw and color a red heart)

repent (draw a red arrow and color the word yellow)

He who has an ear, let him hear what the spirit says to the churches (color it blue)

To him who overcomes (He who overcomes) (overcome) (color yellow)

Satan (devil) (draw a red pitchfork)

second death (underline twice in black)

Seven Spirits of God (draw a purple and color it yellow)

white garments (white robe) (color it yellow)

those who dwell on the earth (color it green)

I looked (I saw) (color it blue)

God (draw a purple triangle and color it yellow)

Throne (draw and color a blue throne)

worthy (color it purple)

worship (circle in purple and color blue)

angel (draw blue wings or a blue angel and color it
   yellow)

book (draw a brown scroll)

seals (on book) (color it orange)

prayers (draw a purple ⌐⌐ ⌐ and color it pink)

wrath (draw a red W)

earthquake (draw a brown ⌇⌇)

seal, sealed (this is different from the seven seals on the
   book) (draw a purple S)

tribulation (box in black)

Remember: Mark WHERE by double-underlining the
WHERE in green. And mark anything that tells you
WHEN by drawing a green clock (L) or a green ○ .

REVELATION 1-7

Chapter 1

1 The Revelation of Jesus Christ, which God gave Him to show to His bond-servants, the things which must soon take place; and He sent and communicated *it* by His angel to His bond-servant John,

2 who testified to the word of God and to the testimony of Jesus Christ, *even* to all that he saw.

3 Blessed is he who reads and those who hear the words of the prophecy, and heed the things which are written in it; for the time is near.

4 John to the seven churches that are in Asia: Grace to you and peace, from Him who is and who was and who is to come, and from the seven Spirits who are before His throne,

5 and from Jesus Christ, the faithful witness, the firstborn of the dead, and the ruler of the kings of the earth. To Him who loves us and released us from our sins by His blood—

6 and He has made us *to be* a kingdom, priests to His God and Father—to Him *be* the glory and the dominion forever and ever. Amen.

7 BEHOLD, HE IS COMING WITH THE CLOUDS, and every eye will

see Him, even those who pierced Him; and all the tribes of the earth will mourn over Him. So it is to be. Amen.

8 "I am the Alpha and the Omega," says the Lord God, "who is and who was and who is to come, the Almighty."

9 I, John, your brother and fellow partaker in the tribulation and kingdom and perseverance *which are* in Jesus, was on the island called Patmos because of the word of God and the testimony of Jesus.

10 I was in the Spirit on the Lord's day, and I heard behind me a loud voice like *the sound* of a trumpet,

11 saying, "Write in a book what you see, and send *it* to the seven churches: to Ephesus and to Smyrna and to Pergamum and to Thyatira and to Sardis and to Philadelphia and to Laodicea."

12 Then I turned to see the voice that was speaking with me. And having turned I saw seven golden lampstands;

13 and in the middle of the lampstands *I saw* one like a son of man, clothed in a robe reaching to the feet, and girded across His chest with a golden sash.

14 His head and His hair were white like white wool, like snow; and His eyes were like a flame of fire.

15 His feet *were* like burnished bronze, when it has been made to glow in a furnace, and His voice *was* like the sound of many waters.

16 In His right hand He held seven stars, and out of His mouth came a sharp two-edged sword; and His face was like the sun shining in its strength.

17 When I saw Him, I fell at His feet like a dead man. And He placed His right hand on me, saying, "Do not be afraid; I am the first and the last,

18 and the living One; and I was dead, and behold, I am alive forevermore, and I have the keys of death and of Hades.

19 "Therefore write the things which you have seen, and the things which are, and the things which will take place after these things.

20 "As for the mystery of the seven stars which you saw in My right hand, and the seven golden lampstands: the seven stars are the angels of the seven churches, and the seven lampstands are the seven churches.

Chapter 2

1 "To the angel of the church in Ephesus write: The One who

holds the seven stars in His right hand, the One who walks

among the seven golden lampstands, says this:

2 'I know your deeds and your toil and perseverance, and that

you cannot tolerate evil men, and you put to the test those who

call themselves apostles, and they are not, and you found them

to be false;

3 and you have perseverance and have endured for My name's

sake, and have not grown weary.

4 'But I have *this* against you, that you have left your first love.

5 'Therefore remember from where you have fallen, and repent

and do the deeds you did at first; or else I am coming to you and

will remove your lampstand out of its place—unless you repent.

6 'Yet this you do have, that you hate the deeds of the

Nicolaitans, which I also hate.

7 'He who has an ear, let him hear what the Spirit says to the

churches. To him who overcomes, I will grant to eat of the tree

of life which is in the Paradise of God.'

8 "And to the angel of the church in Smyrna write:

The first and the last, who was dead, and has come to life, says

this:

9 'I know your tribulation and your poverty (but you are

rich), and the blasphemy by those who say they are Jews and are not, but are a synagogue of Satan.

10 'Do not fear what you are about to suffer. Behold, the devil is about to cast some of you into prison, so that you will be tested, and you will have tribulation for ten days. Be faithful until death, and I will give you the crown of life.

11 'He who has an ear, let him hear what the Spirit says to the churches. He who overcomes will not be hurt by the second death.'

12 "And to the angel of the church in Pergamum write: The One who has the sharp two-edged sword says this:

13 'I know where you dwell, where Satan's throne is; and you hold fast My name, and did not deny My faith even in the days of Antipas, My witness, My faithful one, who was killed among you, where Satan dwells.

14 'But I have a few things against you, because you have there some who hold the teaching of Balaam, who kept teaching Balak to put a stumbling block before the sons of Israel, to eat things sacrificed to idols and to commit *acts of* immorality.

15 'So you also have some who in the same way hold the teaching of the Nicolaitans.

16 'Therefore repent; or else I am coming to you quickly, and I will make war against them with the sword of My mouth.

17 'He who has an ear, let him hear what the Spirit says to the churches. To him who overcomes, to him I will give *some* of the hidden manna, and I will give him a white stone, and a new name written on the stone which no one knows but he who receives it.'

18 "And to the angel of the church in Thyatira write:

The Son of God, who has eyes like a flame of fire, and His feet are like burnished bronze, says this:

19 'I know your deeds, and your love and faith and service and perseverance, and that your deeds of late are greater than at first.

20 'But I have *this* against you, that you tolerate the woman Jezebel, who calls herself a prophetess, and she teaches and leads My bond-servants astray so that they commit *acts of* immorality and eat things sacrificed to idols.

21 'I gave her time to repent, and she does not want to repent of her immorality.

22 'Behold, I will throw her on a bed *of sickness,* and those who

commit adultery with her into great tribulation, unless they repent of her deeds.

23 'And I will kill her children with pestilence, and all the churches will know that I am He who searches the minds and hearts; and I will give to each one of you according to your deeds.

24 'But I say to you, the rest who are in Thyatira, who do not hold this teaching, who have not known the deep things of Satan, as they call them—I place no other burden on you.

25 'Nevertheless what you have, hold fast until I come.

26 'He who overcomes, and he who keeps My deeds until the end, TO HIM I WILL GIVE AUTHORITY OVER THE NATIONS;

27 AND HE SHALL RULE THEM WITH A ROD OF IRON, AS THE VESSELS OF THE POTTER ARE BROKEN TO PIECES, as I also have received *authority* from My Father;

28 and I will give him the morning star.

29 'He who has an ear, let him hear what the Spirit says to the churches.'

Chapter 3

1"To the angel of the church in Sardis write: He who has the seven Spirits of God and the seven stars, says this: 'I know your deeds, that you have a name that you are alive, but you are dead.

2 'Wake up, and strengthen the things that remain, which were about to die; for I have not found your deeds completed in the sight of My God.

3 'So remember what you have received and heard; and keep *it,* and repent. Therefore if you do not wake up, I will come like a thief, and you will not know at what hour I will come to you.

4 'But you have a few people in Sardis who have not soiled their garments; and they will walk with Me in white, for they are worthy.

5 'He who overcomes will thus be clothed in white garments; and I will not erase his name from the book of life, and I will confess his name before My Father and before His angels.

6 'He who has an ear, let him hear what the Spirit says to the churches.'

7 "And to the angel of the church in Philadelphia write: He who is holy, who is true, who has the key of David, who opens and no one will shut, and who shuts and no one opens, says this:

8 'I know your deeds. Behold, I have put before you an open door which no one can shut, because you have a little power, and have kept My word, and have not denied My name.

9 'Behold, I will cause *those* of the synagogue of Satan, who say that they are Jews and are not, but lie—I will make them come and bow down at your feet, and *make them* know that I have loved you.

10 'Because you have kept the word of My perseverance, I also will keep you from the hour of testing, that *hour* which is about to come upon the whole world, to test those who dwell on the earth.

11 'I am coming quickly; hold fast what you have, so that no one will take your crown.

12 'He who overcomes, I will make him a pillar in the temple of My God, and he will not go out from it anymore; and I will write on him the name of My God, and the name of the city of My God, the new Jerusalem, which comes down out of heaven from My God, and My new name.

13 'He who has an ear, let him hear what the Spirit says to the churches.'

14 "To the angel of the church in Laodicea write:

The Amen, the faithful and true Witness, the Beginning of the creation of God, says this:

15 'I know your deeds, that you are neither cold nor hot; I wish that you were cold or hot.

16 'So because you are lukewarm, and neither hot nor cold, I will spit you out of My mouth.

17 'Because you say, "I am rich, and have become wealthy, and have need of nothing," and you do not know that you are wretched and miserable and poor and blind and naked,

18 I advise you to buy from Me gold refined by fire so that you may become rich, and white garments so that you may clothe yourself, and *that* the shame of your nakedness will not be revealed; and eye salve to anoint your eyes so that you may see.

19 'Those whom I love, I reprove and discipline; therefore be zealous and repent.

20 'Behold, I stand at the door and knock; if anyone hears My voice and opens the door, I will come in to him and will dine with him, and he with Me.

21 'He who overcomes, I will grant to him to sit down with Me

on My throne, as I also overcame and sat down with My Father on His throne.

22 'He who has an ear, let him hear what the Spirit says to the churches.'"

Chapter 4

1 After these things I looked, and behold, a door *standing* open in heaven, and the first voice which I had heard, like *the sound* of a trumpet speaking with me, said, "Come up here, and I will show you what must take place after these things."

2 Immediately I was in the Spirit; and behold, a throne was standing in heaven, and One sitting on the throne.

3 And He who was sitting *was* like a jasper stone and a sardius in appearance; and *there was* a rainbow around the throne, like an emerald in appearance.

4 Around the throne *were* twenty-four thrones; and upon the thrones *I saw* twenty-four elders sitting, clothed in white garments, and golden crowns on their heads.

5 Out from the throne come flashes of lightning and sounds and peals of thunder. And *there were* seven lamps of fire

burning before the throne, which are the seven Spirits of God;

6 and before the throne *there was something* like a sea of glass, like crystal; and in the center and around the throne, four living creatures full of eyes in front and behind.

7 The first creature *was* like a lion, and the second creature like a calf, and the third creature had a face like that of a man, and the fourth creature *was* like a flying eagle.

8 And the four living creatures, each one of them having six wings, are full of eyes around and within; and day and night they do not cease to say,

"HOLY, HOLY, HOLY *is* THE LORD GOD, THE ALMIGHTY, WHO WAS AND WHO IS AND WHO IS TO COME."

9 And when the living creatures give glory and honor and thanks to Him who sits on the throne, to Him who lives forever and ever,

10 the twenty-four elders will fall down before Him who sits on the throne, and will worship Him who lives forever and ever, and will cast their crowns before the throne, saying,

11 "Worthy are You, our Lord and our God, to receive glory and

honor and power; for You created all things, and because of Your will they existed, and were created."

Chapter 5

1 I saw in the right hand of Him who sat on the throne a book written inside and on the back, sealed up with seven seals.

2 And I saw a strong angel proclaiming with a loud voice, "Who is worthy to open the book and to break its seals?"

3 And no one in heaven or on the earth or under the earth was able to open the book or to look into it.

4 Then I *began* to weep greatly because no one was found worthy to open the book or to look into it;

5 and one of the elders said to me, "Stop weeping; behold, the Lion that is from the tribe of Judah, the Root of David, has overcome so as to open the book and its seven seals."

6 And I saw between the throne (with the four living creatures) and the elders a Lamb standing, as if slain, having seven horns and seven eyes, which are the seven Spirits of God, sent out into all the earth.

7 And He came and took the book out of the right hand of Him who sat on the throne.

8 When He had taken the book, the four living creatures and the twenty-four elders fell down before the Lamb, each one holding a harp and golden bowls full of incense, which are the prayers of the saints.

9 And they sang a new song, saying, "Worthy are You to take the book and to break its seals; for You were slain, and purchased for God with Your blood *men* from every tribe and tongue and people and nation.

10 "You have made them *to be* a kingdom and priests to our God; and they will reign upon the earth."

11 Then I looked, and I heard the voice of many angels around the throne and the living creatures and the elders; and the number of them was myriads of myriads, and thousands of thousands,

12 saying with a loud voice, "Worthy is the Lamb that was slain to receive power and riches and wisdom and might and honor and glory and blessing."

13 And every created thing which is in heaven and on the earth and under the earth and on the sea, and all things in

them, I heard saying, "To Him who sits on the throne, and to the Lamb, *be* blessing and honor and glory and dominion forever and ever."

14 And the four living creatures kept saying, "Amen." And the elders fell down and worshiped.

Chapter 6

1 Then I saw when the Lamb broke one of the seven seals, and I heard one of the four living creatures saying as with a voice of thunder, "Come."

2 I looked, and behold, a white horse, and he who sat on it had a bow; and a crown was given to him, and he went out conquering and to conquer.

3 When He broke the second seal, I heard the second living creature saying, "Come."

4 And another, a red horse, went out; and to him who sat on it, it was granted to take peace from the earth, and that *men* would slay one another; and a great sword was given to him.

5 When He broke the third seal, I heard the third living creature saying, "Come." I looked, and behold, a black horse; and he who sat on it had a pair of scales in his hand.

6 And I heard *something* like a voice in the center of the four living creatures saying, "A quart of wheat for a denarius, and three quarts of barley for a denarius; and do not damage the oil and the wine."

7 When the Lamb broke the fourth seal, I heard the voice of the fourth living creature saying, "Come."

8 I looked, and behold, an ashen horse; and he who sat on it had the name Death; and Hades was following with him. Authority was given to them over a fourth of the earth, to kill with sword and with famine and with pestilence and by the wild beasts of the earth.

9 When the Lamb broke the fifth seal, I saw underneath the altar the souls of those who had been slain because of the word of God, and because of the testimony which they had maintained; 10 and they cried out with a loud voice, saying, "How long, O Lord, holy and true, will You refrain from judging and avenging our blood on those who dwell on the earth?"

11 And there was given to each of them a white robe; and they were told that they should rest for a little while longer, until *the number of* their fellow servants and their brethren who were to be killed even as they had been, would be completed also.

12 I looked when He broke the sixth seal, and there was a great earthquake; and the sun became black as sackcloth *made* of hair, and the whole moon became like blood;

13 and the stars of the sky fell to the earth, as a fig tree casts its unripe figs when shaken by a great wind.

14 The sky was split apart like a scroll when it is rolled up, and every mountain and island were moved out of their places.

15 Then the kings of the earth and the great men and the commanders and the rich and the strong and every slave and free man hid themselves in the caves and among the rocks of the mountains;

16 and they said to the mountains and to the rocks, "Fall on us and hide us from the presence of Him who sits on the throne, and from the wrath of the Lamb;

17 for the great day of their wrath has come, and who is able to stand?"

Chapter 7

1 After this I saw four angels standing at the four corners of the earth, holding back the four winds of the earth, so that no wind would blow on the earth or on the sea or on any tree.

2 And I saw another angel ascending from the rising of the sun, having the seal of the living God; and he cried out with a loud voice to the four angels to whom it was granted to harm the earth and the sea,

3 saying, "Do not harm the earth or the sea or the trees until we have sealed the bond-servants of our God on their foreheads."

4 And I heard the number of those who were sealed, one hundred and forty-four thousand sealed from every tribe of the sons of Israel:

5 from the tribe of Judah, twelve thousand *were* sealed, from the tribe of Reuben twelve thousand, from the tribe of Gad twelve thousand,

6 from the tribe of Asher twelve thousand, from the tribe of Naphtali twelve thousand, from the tribe of Manasseh twelve thousand,

7 from the tribe of Simeon twelve thousand, from the tribe of Levi twelve thousand, from the tribe of Issachar twelve thousand,

8 from the tribe of Zebulun twelve thousand, from the tribe

of Joseph twelve thousand, from the tribe of Benjamin, twelve thousand *were* sealed.

9 After these things I looked, and behold, a great multitude which no one could count, from every nation and *all* tribes and peoples and tongues, standing before the throne and before the Lamb, clothed in white robes, and palm branches *were* in their hands;

10 and they cry out with a loud voice, saying, "Salvation to our God who sits on the throne, and to the Lamb."

11 And all the angels were standing around the throne and *around* the elders and the four living creatures; and they fell on their faces before the throne and worshiped God,

12 saying,

"Amen, blessing and glory and wisdom and thanksgiving and honor and power and might, *be* to our God forever and ever. Amen."

13 Then one of the elders answered, saying to me, "These who are clothed in the white robes, who are they, and where have they come from?"

14 I said to him, "My lord, you know." And he said to me, "These are the ones who come out of the great tribulation,

and they have washed their robes and made them white in the blood of the Lamb.

15 "For this reason, they are before the throne of God; and they serve Him day and night in His temple; and He who sits on the throne will spread His tabernacle over them.

16 "They will hunger no longer, nor thirst anymore; nor will the sun beat down on them, nor any heat;

17 for the Lamb in the center of the throne will be their shepherd, and will guide them to springs of the water of life; and God will wipe every tear from their eyes."